Multicore Hardware-Software Design and Verification Techniques

Edited By

Pao-Ann Hsiung

*Department of Computer Science and Information Engineering,
National Chung Cheng University, Taiwan*

Yean-Ru Chen

*Graduate Institute of Electronic Engineering,
National Taiwan University, Taiwan*

Chao-Sheng Lin

*Department of Computer Science and Information Engineering,
National Chung Cheng University, Taiwan*

DEDICATION

My wife Nancy, daughters Alice, Phoebe, Tiffany and last, but not the least, my son Roger

Pao-Ann Hsiung

My parents, grandparents, and ToYu

Yean-Ru Chen

My parents and VMC Members

Chao-Sheng Lin

CONTENTS

CHAPTERS

FOREWORD

Though the transistor density in a single chip keeps doubling every 18 months according to the Moore's law from 1965, the increasing of clock frequency has hit its ceiling owing to physical constraints around 2003. Memory wall, instruction-level parallelism (ILP) wall, and power wall are the main obstacles for high clock speed in a microprocessor. To overcome the barriers and keep exploiting the advantages from Moore's law, microprocessor vendors have started providing multi-core architectures that can increase the computing power for application acceleration. Today multi-core architectures have been proved to be ideal solutions by being adopted in a wide range from the server, desktop, and laptop to the embedded systems and digital signal processing design.

Though multi-core systems have brought us the benefits of higher computing power and low power consumption, it has also created new challenges in hardware architecture design and software application design and analysis. For the hardware architecture, the design of memory distribution and cache hierarchy is important, which may affect the cache hit rate, memory access latency, thread scheduling, and migration strategies. For software design, operating systems, parallel algorithms and libraries, and language extensions are being developed to support parallel programming models based the multi-threaded programming paradigm. Application designers need to analyze the computationally intensive tasks in an application and decompose them into smaller logical tasks to be managed by parallel algorithms (libraries). All the issues arising from each design level may affect the application performance on multi-core systems.

This ebook, *Multicore Hardware-Software Design and Verification Techniques*, tries to give the readership an overview on the major issues of engineering in multi-core systems and the inception of marching into the multi-core world. Chapters 1, 2, and 3 help readers to assimilate the major issues in system design due to the characteristics of diverse multi-core architectures. Chapters 4 and 5 introduce the issues in application design and analysis, which are targeted for multi-core systems. This book is designed to give the readers a consolidated and hierarchal concept from the underlying multi-core architectural characteristics to the high-level software and application design. I believe readers will not only learn from this book, but will be of high reference value.

Ahmed Jerraya
CEA-LETI, MINATEC
France

PREFACE

The surge of multicore processors coming into the market and on users' desktops has made parallel computing the focus of attention once again. At this focal point of urgency and immaturity, this e-book is being put forward as a platform for immediate collection of state-of-the-art technologies in both hardware and software designs for multicore computing.

READERSHIP

It is our hope that this ebook will be of immense help to system and software engineers, including both experts and non-experts in multicore processor design and software programming. Potential readership is as follows:

1. The vast majority of software programmers who are perplexed by the rapidly increasing number of cores in a processor and by the parallel computing techniques required of them

2. Educators in the hardware and software fields, who need to catch up with multicore programming so that engineers entering the industry already have the basic art of parallel computing

3. Researchers in the parallel computing field, who need to ensure that their background knowledge in parallel computing can be adapted to multiple on-chip cores and not only distributed computing clusters

There are totally five chapters included in this ebook, which were selected from a number of submissions and reviewed thoroughly. Some of the chapters were invited from prominent groups of researchers. The chapters mainly deal with issues of thread scheduling, energy saving, and model-driven software generation and verification. In the following, we will briefly describe each of the chapters included in this issue of the ebook.

ORGANIZATION

The first chapter focuses on thread scheduling for many-core architectures that are interconnected by a 2-dimensional mesh interconnection network. It mainly evaluates thread scheduling and migration techniques through simulation. Core affinity and distance-based migration are the main criteria proposed for high-performance scheduling.

The second chapter focuses on *green* design with performance improvement for the cache designs in multi-core systems. It evaluates where to place the miss table in a multi-level cache hierarchy. For MPEG4 and FFT algorithms, the authors claim that cache locking at level-1 is more beneficiary than at level-2. Not only is the mean delay per task reduced significantly, but the total power consumption is also reduced drastically.

The third chapter is another chapter on *green* design, which focuses on how tag reduction for level-1 instruction cache can be performed in multi-core systems. A significant amount of power is saved by the proposed Tag Reduction on CMP (TRoCMP) method.

The fourth chapter is about a multi-core embedded software development framework called VERTAF/Multi-Core (VMC), which encompasses all phases of the design flow, including requirements modeling, design modeling, architecture mapping, code generation, code optimization, testing, and multi-view design repository. Automatic model-driven software development is the main goal of VMC. This is also an open-source project, which has resulted in software tools that are available for research and academia.

The fifth and final chapter in this ebook is mainly about how code can be automatically generated from SysML models that contain user-specified parallelism. All three real-world parallelism, including task parallelism, data parallelism, and data-flow parallelism (such as parallel pipeline) have been addressed in the code generator. The code generator has also been integrated as a part of the VMC framework. Currently, it supports multiple multi-core platforms including ARM 11 MPCore and Intel quad core. Libraries such as *quantum platform* (QP) for realizing state machines and Intel's threading building block (TBB) for realizing parallelism are both supported in the VMC code generator.

EDITOR BIOGRAPHIES

Pao-Ann Hsiung, Ph.D., received his B.S. in Mathematics and his Ph.D. in Electrical Engineering from the National Taiwan University, Taipei, Taiwan, ROC, in 1991 and 1996, respectively. From 1996 to 2000, he was a post-doctoral researcher at the Institute of Information Science, Academia Sinica, Taipei, Taiwan, ROC. From February 2001 to July 2002, he was an assistant professor and from August 2002 to July 2007 he was an associate professor in the Department of Computer Science and Information Engineering, National Chung Cheng University, Chiayi, Taiwan, ROC. Since August 2007, he has been a full professor.

Dr. Hsiung was the recipient of the 2001 ACM Taipei Chapter Kuo-Ting Li Young Researcher for his significant contributions to design automation of electronic systems. Dr. Hsiung was also a recipient of the 2004 Young Scholar Research Award given by National Chung Cheng University to five young faculty members per year.

Dr. Hsiung is a senior member of the IEEE, a senior member of the ACM, and a life member of the IICM. He has been included in several professional listings such as Marquis' Who's Who in the World, Marquis' Who's Who in Asia, Outstanding People of the 20th Century by International Biographical Centre, Cambridge, England, Rifacimento International's Admirable Asian Achievers (2006), Afro/Asian Who's Who, and Asia/Pacific Who's Who. Dr. Hsiung is an editorial board member of the International Journal of Embedded Systems (IJES), Inderscience Publishers, USA; the International Journal of Multimedia and Ubiquitous Engineering (IJMUE), Science and Engineering Research Center (SERSC), USA; an associate editor of the Journal of Software Engineering (JSE), Academic Journals, Inc., USA; an editorial board member of the Open Software Engineering Journal (OSE), Bentham Science Publishers, Ltd., USA; an international editorial board member of the International Journal of Patterns (IJOP). Dr. Hsiung has been on the program committee of more than 60 international conferences. He served as session organizer and chair for PDPTA'99, and as workshop organizer and chair for RTC'99, DSVV'2000, PDES'2005, WoRMES'2009, and WESQA'2010. He has published more than 200 papers in international journals and conferences. He has taken an active part in paper refereeing for international journals and conferences.

His main research interests include multi-core programming, reconfigurable computing and system design, cognitive radio architecture, System-on-Chip (SoC) design and verification, embedded software synthesis and verification, real-time system design and verification, hardware-software codesign and coverification, and component-based object-oriented application frameworks for real-time embedded systems.

Yean-Ru Chen received the B.S. degree in Computer Science and Information Engineering from the National Chiao Tung University, Hsinchu, Taiwan, ROC in 2002. From 2002 to 2003, she was employed as an engineer in SoC Technology Center, Industrial Technology Research Institute, Hsinchu, Taiwan, ROC. She received the M.S. degree in Computer Science and Information Engineering from the National Chung Cheng University, ChiaYi, Taiwan, ROC in 2006. She is currently a Ph.D. candidate in Graduate Institute of Electronics Engineering of National Taiwan University, Taipei, Taiwan, ROC.

Her current research interests include model checking, SAT, SMT, safety-critical systems, network-on-chip (NoC), security-critical systems (role-based access systems) and Multi-Core embedded software.

Chao-Sheng Lin received the B.S. degree in Architecture and Urban Design from Chinese Culture University, Taipei, Taiwan, ROC, in 1998, and the M.S. degree in the Department of Computer Science and Information Engineering from National Chung Cheng University, Chiayi, Taiwan, ROC, in 2007. He is now working toward the PhD degree in the Department of Computer Science and Information Engineering at National Chung Cheng University. He has two-year working experience in software engineering and had been the vice senior software engineer in Synchronous Communication Corp. in Taiwan.

His research interests include formal verification, reconfigurable systems, and multi-core programming.

ACKNOWLEDGMENTS

We greatly appreciate the contributions from all the authors and thanks to Bentham Science Publishers for providing us such great opportunity to publish this ebook.

Pao-Ann Hsiung
Department of Computer Science and Information Engineering
National Chung Cheng University
Taiwan

Yean-Ru Chen
Graduate Institute of Electronic Engineering
National Taiwan University
Taiwan

&

Chao-Sheng Lin
Department of Computer Science and Information Engineering
National Chung Cheng University
Taiwan

LIST OF CONTRIBUTORS

Abu Asaduzzaman   *Department of Computer and Electrical Engineering and Computer Science, Florida Atlantic University, Boca Raton, Florida 33431, USA.*

Chih-Hung Chang   *Department of Information Management, Hsiuping Institute of Technology, Taichung, Taiwan*

Yi-Luen Chang   *Department of Computer Science and Information Engineering, National Chung Cheng University, Taiwan.*

William C.-C. Chu   *Department of Computer Science, Tunghai University, Taichung, Taiwan.*

Mianxiong Dong   *School of Computer Science and Engineering, University of Aizu, Aizu-Wakamatsu, 965-8580, Japan.*

Department of Electrical and Computer Engineering, University of Waterloo, Waterloo, N2L, 3G1, Canada.

Minyi Guo   *Department of Computer Science and Engineering, Shanghai Jiao Tong University, Shanghai, 200020, China*

Song Guo   *School of Computer Science and Engineering, University of Aizu, Aizu-Wakamatsu, 965-8580, Japan.*

Chia-Chiao Ho   *Department of Computer Science and Information Engineering, National Chung Cheng University, Taiwan.*

Pao-Ann Hsiung   *Department of Computer Science and Information Engineering, National Chung Cheng University, Taiwan.*

Nien-Lin Hsueh   *Department of Computer Science and Information Engineering, Feng Chia University, Taichung, Taiwan.*

Chorng-Shiuh Koong   *Department of Computer and Information Science, National Taichung University, Taichung, Taiwan.*

Shang-Wei Lin   *Department of Computer Science and Information Engineering, National Chung Cheng University, Taiwan.*

Chao-Sheng Lin   *Department of Computer Science and Information Engineering, National Chung Cheng University, Taiwan.*

Yu-Shin Lin   *Department of Computer Science and Information Engineering, National Chung Cheng University, Taiwan.*

Chun-Hsien Lu   *Department of Computer Science and Information Engineering, National Chung Cheng University, Taiwan.*

Jun Ma   *School of Computer Science and Engineering, University of Aizu, Aizu-Wakamatsu, 965-8580, Japan*

Kaoru Ota   *School of Computer Science and Engineering, University of Aizu, Aizu-Wakamatsu, 965-8580, Japan*

Department of Electrical and Computer Engineering, University of Waterloo, Waterloo, N2L, 3G1, Canada.

Fadi N. Sibai   *Faculty of Information Technology, UAE University, P. O. Box 17551, Al Ain, United Arab Emirates.*

Chih-Hsiong Shih   *Department of Computer Science, Tunghai University, Taichung, Taiwan.*

Bo-Hsuan Wang   *Department of Computer Science and Information Engineering, National Chung Cheng University, Taiwan.*

Chao-Tung Yang   *Department of Computer Science, Tunghai University, Taichung, Taiwan.*

Long Zheng   *School of Computer Science and Engineering, University of Aizu, Aizu-Wakamatsu, 965-8580, Japan.*

School of Computer Science and Technology, Huazhong University of Science and Technology, 430074, China.

ACKNOWLEDGEMENTS

This ebook has benefited immensely from review by a number of people who gave generously of their time and expertise. The following professors provided detailed technical reviews of all the chapters (listed in alphabetical order with the affiliations):

- Dr, Chih-Hung Chang (Dept. of Information Management, Hsiuping Institute of Technology, Taiwan),

- Dr. Trong-Yen Lee (Dept. of Electronic Engineering, National Taipei University of Technology, Taiwan) and

- Dr. Adam Porter (Dept. of Computer Science, University of Maryland, USA),

- Dr. Zili Shao (Dept. of Computing, The Hong Kong Polytechnic University, Hong Kong),

- Dr. Chihhsiong Shih (Dept. of Computer Science and Information Engineering, Tunghai University, Taiwan).

We also thank the many people responsible for publication of this ebook. This includes the staffs at Bentham Science Publishers.

CHAPTER 1

Affinity and Distance-Aware Thread Scheduling and Migration in Reconfigurable Many-Core Architectures

Fadi N. Sibai*

Faculty of Information Technology, UAE University, P. O. Box 17551, Al Ain, United Arab Emirates

Abstract: Modern many-core CMPs and MPSoC embedded systems integrate different cores. A 2D mesh interconnects the routers at each core providing system reconfigurability which for instance allows the bypassing of specific routes due to faults or congestion. In this work, a class-based many-core architecture with reconfigurable classes and a 2D Mesh-based on-chip interconnection network is considered. We present an affinity- and distance-aware thread scheduling scheme and migration policies for a reconfigurable heterogeneous class-based 2D Mesh-interconnected many-core CMP. We also present a simulator for evaluating various scheduling and migration algorithms. The simulation results reveal that scheduling algorithms which both consider core affinity and support distance-based migration outperform the other considered algorithms in reconfigurable many-core architectures.

INTRODUCTION

Heterogeneous or asymmetric many-core (AMC) processors –aka chip multiprocessors or CMPs--, multiprocessor systems on chip (MPSoCs), as well as symmetric many-core architectures (SMC) are becoming pervasive [1-3]. Most of the commercial offerings have been symmetric ranging from x86 offerings from Intel and AMD, to Sun T1. The IBM Cell [2] is an exception with the integration of a PowerPC host core with 8 identical Synergistic Processing Element cores which qualifies it for the heterogeneous attribute. SMCs integrate identical CPU cores with identical capabilities and features onto one processor die. They are a great fit to workloads with roughly equivalent threads with similar computation requirements. Realistic workloads with a mix of applications, background tasks, and operating system all running simultaneously are typically composed of threads of different computation and time requirements, some running at an adequate performance level with simple low-power ALUs while others needing more advanced power-consuming vectorized ALUs and predictors. Some threads run better alone as they avoid costly interference in shared resources when run simultaneously, while other threads run better together at the same time when scheduled on the same simultaneous multithreading processor [4].

The asymmetric kind has performance/watt advantages despite the fact that the symmetric kind may offer better redundancy and may be easier to design. Simply said, AMCs may better serve and fit the basket of active threads with their various functionality and performance requirements than the uniform SMC kind.

MPSoCs integrate many cores on the same chip interconnected by a network-on-chip (NoC) or on-chip interconnection network (OCIN) and are heterogeneous in nature.

A very important effector of performance is the thread schedule, and more precisely, the thread scheduling algorithm which has been widely researched and is as important as ever with the increasing number of cores in many-cores. Scheduling algorithms seek to optimize various metrics but an important one has been and remains the completion time of a group of threads. In real-time embedded systems, scheduling seeks to meet real time targets. In many-cores, due to the ample hardware resources available per chip, it makes sense to migrate threads to remote cores from the ones on which they ran last if these latter ones are unavailable rather than force them to wait in queues. One goal of the migration policy is to determine the remote core to which a thread can migrate with minimum moving or transfer costs.

One effective way to evaluate the performance of thread scheduling algorithms and migration policies is *via* simulation. A simulator only implements the pieces relevant to performance while abstracting the rest, and hence

*Address correspondence to Dr. Fadi N. Sibai:** Faculty of Information Technology, UAE University, P. O. Box 17551, Al Ain, United Arab Emirates; Tel: +971-3-7135589; E-mail: fadi.sibai@uaeu.ac.ae

can give an accurate answer and provide meaningful comparisons of various algorithms, policies and various system parameters at low cost and in short time.

In this Chapter, we present a distance-based scheduling algorithm and thread scheduling simulator for a class-based mesh-connected many-core processor. We also consider various thread scheduling algorithms and migration policies. The simulation environment which we developed can evaluate the performance of various migration policies in conjunction with a custom-made thread scheduling algorithm for a particular AMC. We review the latest scheduling schemes proposed for many-cores in the next section. In the section following it, we briefly describe a 16-core version of the AMC architecture. Next, the priority-based round robin scheduling algorithm for that AMC architecture is described. The section which follows it describes the simulation model and all considered migration policies and presents the simulation results. We then address the implications of system and NoC reconfigurability on the performance of the scheduling algorithms and migration policies considered and then conclude the Chapter.

SCHEDULING SCHEMES FOR CMPs

Multi-/Many-core processors or Chip Multiprocessors (CMPs) [5] are now prevalent and omnipresent. As the number of cores becomes large, many designs share large resources to cut down on cost and power consumption. Several commercial CMPs are available on the market [2, 6-8] ranging from 2 to 16 cores per chip. Thread scheduling is an important topic as threads translate into thousands of processor clocks.

Some of the important issues relevant to CMPs are single thread migration [9-11], shared resource partitioning among co-scheduled threads and cache fair scheduling. Hily & Seznec [12] point to a strong link between 2nd level (L2) cache contention and thread performance. Balakrishnan et al [13] analyzed the stability and scalability of commercial server workloads on asymmetric cores and found that asymmetry hurts performance predictability and scalability and recommended making both the operating system kernel and the application aware of the hardware asymmetry in order to circumvent these issues. Kim et al [14] recommends making both the operating system and the application aware of the hardware asymmetry in case of AMC. Fair cache sharing and partitioning [14] was found to optimize throughput in CMPs. Chandra et al [15] proposed and evaluated 3 models for predicting the impact of cache sharing on co-scheduled threads. Another cache fair scheduling algorithm for CMPs was proposed in [16-17]. The idea is to give larger time slices to co-scheduled threads that suffer more from extra L2 cache misses due to being scheduled with other threads.

Scheduling is an old and important research area that is revisited when new architectural directions are taken which can benefit from other scheduling ideas. A survey of scheduling algorithm can be found in [18-19]. The benefits of affinity and page migration in multiprocessor scheduling has been shown in [20] who demonstrated better processor utilization with space-sharing (space means resource) policies and user data distribution helping time-slicing policies. Chandra et al [20] analyzed various scheduling algorithms and explored cache and cluster affinities [21-23] and cluster affinity in a ccNUMA architecture and a page migration based on DTLB misses. They found that the winning policy changes from application to another and across data distributions. Another scheduling idea is gang scheduling [24] which schedules the threads of an application to run simultaneously with benefits to communication and synchronization times. A 2-level scheduler was proposed in [25].

Scheduling algorithms can be classified into resource-based and sampling-based algorithms. Resource-based algorithms are those which optimize resource utilization or thread balance and make scheduling decisions based on resource utilization and thread balance. Among these algorithms are those which allow thread to migrate from core to core in order to exploit available resources or to distribute the load evenly among cores, those which allow data pages to migrate from core to core to reduce cache and TLB latencies and cache coherence traffic including false sharing, and those which allow both thread and data migration.

Sampling-based scheduling algorithms periodically sample some performance event counters which are monitored such as IPC and cache misses. Examples of such algorithms were described in [26-28]. In [26], a number of threads with the highest metric (performance event count) values are scheduled together, where metrics varied from IPC, L2 cache miss rates, L1 data cache misses to DTLB misses and number of branch mispredictions, all per thread. Their evaluation analysis with SPEC95 revealed the IPC metric to provide the highest speedup with up to 15% gain over standard round robin scheduling. It turns out that scheduling the threads with the lowest L2 miss rate indeed generated a workload execution with the minimum L2 misses; however it also generated the highest L1 cache misses among the rest. In that perspective, the sampling-based algorithms which made decision based on L1 or L2 misses, DTLB misses and number of mispredictions ended up not being the best as they fixed one metric but hurt another. The scheduling decision based on minimizing the IPC ended up being the best option as it sought to maximize the workload throughput. Parekh [26] 's thread-sensitive scheduling technique did not prevent starvation. It is also interesting to note that affinity, unlike in multi-core architectures, did not help the performance of simultaneous multithreaded processors (SMT) as all threads shared the cache memories. On multi-core architectures with L1 cache memories private to the cores, and higher cache memories shared by either a subset of the totality of the cores, the situation is very much different.

Bulpin & Pratt [27] used the results of [26] to develop a scheduler based on IPC for hyper-threaded Intel-based systems running Linux. In reality they evaluate the process' throughput as the execution rate under hyper-threading versus its execution rate without hyper-threading when all the core's resources are available to the process. They modify the goodness function to calculate the dynamic priority of a task when scheduling tasks, where the task with the highest goodness value corresponding to the highest IPC is executed.

Symbiotic scheduling [28] sampled various job combinations and recorded performance metrics for each job combination. Symbiosis refers to the group of threads which can run together with the minimal interference thus hurting each other's performance the least. [10] presented a vector-based technique for data migration and thread migration to reduce global communication distances and to enhance resource demand distribution among the system's resources. Data migration seeks to localize the data to reduce data fetching costs while thread migration seeks to achieve a thread execution balance. They argue that with the advent of the multi-core or CMP age, data and threads do not have to reside on the same core but can be in nearby on-chip cores within acceptable latency times. By moving data and threads to nearby cores, the on-chip communication slightly increases while resource demands are more balanced. They define: i. an attraction vector for each data or thread which conveys the data or thread's inter-core communication direction; and ii. a repulsion vector associated with specific core regions or partitions which conveys the direction that a thread or data should move towards. A migration vector combining the latter 2 vectors is then computed to tell where the thread or data should move to, given that 2 vectors in opposing directions cancel each other. They assume such migration to repeat every 10K cycles and that migration computation based on the above vector computations takes only 100 processor cycles. On an application such as Ray tracing which benefits from data locality and resource balancing a 64% reduction in execution time was observed while on other applications with dissimilar characteristics no gains were observed.

DeVuyst et al [29] proposed sampling-based scheduling that considers power in its decision making. Unlike our algorithm, they assume that all threads have equal priorities. They evaluate sampling-based scheduling and electron-based (repelling and attracting based on contention or availability) scheduling policies with the SPEC2000 benchmark. On a single simultaneous multithreading (SMT) core, performance drops while energy is maximized as threads are added. A delicate balance must be reached by the scheduler to achieve the best of performance and energy. When scheduling for best performance and power, [29] found that the best policy changes across workloads and thus recommend adaptable scheduling which changes according to the workload.

In the next sections, we briefly describe the AMC architecture on which we conduct thread scheduling and migration simulations, followed by a nearest neighbor distance-based and core affinity-based thread scheduling algorithm. We then sketch for this scheduling scheme various migration policies and describe the simulator which simulates and compares the performance of thread schedule runs under each of these scheduling and migration policies. In this study, we assume that thread migration incurs a time penalty which our simulation environment accounts for. We also assume that threads have different priorities and serve them according to their priorities while avoiding thread starvation. Our scheduling algorithm employs a nearest neighbor migration policy which minimizes thread migration costs by migrating the thread to the nearest possible available core (inter-core distance aware) with minimum required functionality (core class). Core migration in our scheme is not just limited to the North, South, East or West core neighbors can even cross core classes. Finally, our algorithm is adaptable by allowing the operating system to set a few parameters based on the workload conditions.

ASYMMETRIC MANY-CORE ARCHITECTURE

In this section, we review an asymmetric many-core (AMC) architecture with four core classes, selected as such to provide a wide range of workload support. Each class contains cores with various functionality in order to maximize performance per watt and in order to avoid whenever possible allocating more power consuming cores with higher functionality to applications which do not need that functionality. In this Chapter, we consider 4 classes in order to provide a large enough choice to various workloads while still fitting within the total number of cores which is 16. The number of core classes is flexible and can be modified according to varying needs thus supporting system reconfigurability. In addition, each core is associated with a network router and routers are interconnected *via* a 2D mesh network with Manhattan-style routing. The use of routers provides system reconfigurability, for instance allows the bypassing of specific routes due to faulty cores or links or congestion at specific router ports. Thus the number of classes is reconfigurable in theory as well as the inter-core paths or routes. The number of classes and size of classes can be reconfigured to best suit the active workload. In our AMC architecture, we consider the following 4 classes:

   i.   Class A: high power, high ILP, complex predictors, vector execution units (supporting SIMD instruction sets such as MMx or SSE or Altivec), large L2 cache;

   ii. Class B: medium power and ILP, vector execution units, medium L2 cache;

   iii. Class C: low power and ILP, small L2 cache; and

   iv. Class D: special purpose cores (media codecs, encryption, I/O processor).

Fig. **1** shows an instance or the proposed AMC architecture with 16 cores and 4 classes. The AMC architecture is reconfigurable and can support different number of core classes and/or various numbers of cores per class. In this particular instance or implementation of the AMC architecture, each of the first 3 classes is divided in half between single threaded processors (with even numbers) and multi-threaded processors (with odd core numbers).

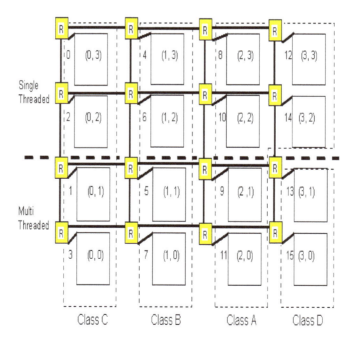

Figure 1: AMC architecture.

Note that this multithread/single-thread division is not absolutely necessary and may be omitted in some implementations. In a 16-core processor, a core ID identifies a core where the least significant bit identifies it as singled threaded or multi-threaded. By mixing cores with various power requirements and computational capabilities, it is intended to maximize the probability of good mapping of wide workloads into the AMC's cores. Furthermore, this asymmetric architecture makes the process of cut and paste of existing core easy and maximizes performance per watt. Note that cores in the lower classes (e.g. C) miss some of the functionality of cores in the higher classes (e.g. A). Contrary to what is pictured in Fig. **1**, the core areas of the various classes are unequal and class A cores occupy much larger areas that class C cores. When a thread is scheduled for the 1st time, if the thread only requires a single threaded class C core (cores 0 or 2) and neither is available, then the scheduling algorithm (that we'll discuss in the next section) will select an available core in the nearest higher class possible, and specifically in the following order: multi-threaded class C (cores 1 or 3), single-threaded class B (cores 4 or 6), multi-threaded class B (cores 5 or 7), single-threaded class A (cores 8, 10, 12, or 14), and finally multi-threaded class A (cores 9 or 11). Note that class D cores (13 and 15) have special functions and normal threads are not mapped to them but special operations are assigned to class D cores. However if a thread requiring a multi-threaded class B core finds none to be available, then the scheduler will attempt to schedule it to a single threaded class A core if one is available. If none are available, the scheduler cannot make an assignment to an available core in the lower class C as these do not support some required functionality (e.g. vector units) and so the thread is requeued and not scheduled.

On a 2nd or later attempt to schedule a thread, the scheduler attempts to assign a thread to run on the core on which it ran the last time it got scheduled thus satisfying the core affinity of the thread to minimize inter-core thread state update overhead penalties. For instance if a thread previously ran on core 2 in Class C and is later rescheduled, the scheduling algorithm attempts to assign it to core 2 again, and if not available to the nearest core in Class C as illustrated in Figs. **2** and **3a**. The top priorities are cores 2, 0 (single-threaded as core 2), 1 and 3 in class C. When no class C core is available, the thread is migrated to one of the class B classes according to the priority order of Fig. **3b**. In Fig. **3**, the numbers represent core numbers while the arrows represent thread migrations labeled with their priorities. Priority Pi is higher than priority Pj when i<j. When neither class C or B core is available, the thread is migrated to one of the core A cores according to the priority order of Fig. **3c**.

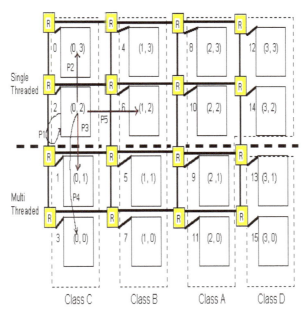

Figure 2: Destination core priorities in the same core class.

In mesh-connected AMCs, it is desirable to schedule cooperating threads to as close cores as possible in order to minimize the communication time. The distance form $core_i$ to $core_j$ is given by

$$Distance(core_i, core_j) = |x_j - x_i| + |y_j - y_i| \qquad (1)$$

where $core_i$ = CPU core i's number, and its 2D coordinates (x_i, y_i) are given by

$$x_i = \lfloor core_i / 4 \rfloor \quad y_i = (core_i \bmod 4) \text{ if } y_i \in \{0, 3\} \text{ then } y_i = (y_i + 3) \bmod 6 \qquad (2)$$

As these may involve three costly divisions, it is desirable to create a table of inter-core distances for each core that includes cores in the same class or in higher classes. For instance for core 5, 1-hop cores include cores in the set {7, 6, 9}, 2-hop cores include core in {4, 11, 10}, 3-hop cores include cores in {8}.

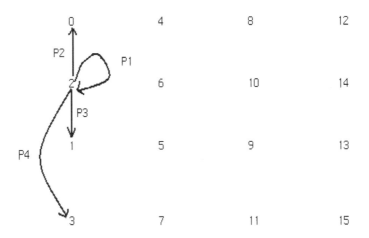

a. Migration priorities in the same class.

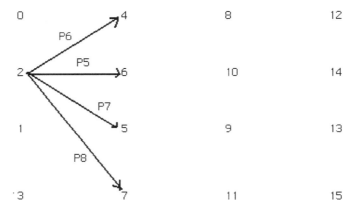

b. Migration priorities in the immediately higher class.

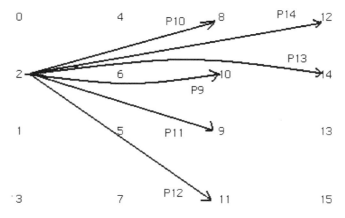

c. Migration priorities in the next higher class.

Figure 3: Destination core priorities.

SCHEDULING SCHEME FOR AMC

Scheduling algorithms attempt to deliver schedules which optimize metrics such as maximum throughput, minimum response time, minimum waiting time, or maximum CPU utilization [18, 19]. Several algorithms exist such as shortest job first, round robin, etc, each with its advantages and drawbacks. Since tasks have different priorities, some that need urgent attention while others have more tolerance for waiting, it makes sense for the scheduling algorithm to be priority-based. While optimal schedules are desired, it is also important to avoid excessive data collection and intensive schedule computation in order to keep the scheduling overhead time under control.

While hardware features and compiler optimizations may greatly benefit a program's performance, a scheduling algorithm tailored for the architecture it targets can bring even higher benefits. Scheduling a thread with another thread on a dual core processor can be performance-disastrous if both threads simultaneously contend for insufficiently available shared resources. Even worse expectations can result from the operating system scheduler scheduling lower priority tasks before higher priority ones.

In a priority-based scheduling scheme, each thread is assigned a priority either by the programmer (*via* system API) or the operating system. Several scheduling queues exist one for each priority. The scheduler attempts to schedule threads waiting in the highest priority queue 1 first, followed by those in priority queue 2, etc. Priority-based schedulers can cause starvation for the lower priority threads. Some avoidance policies enforce aging which increases the priority of threads as time progresses thus each queued thread will eventually reach highest priority if not scheduled. Others allocate time slices to each queue which distributes its allotted time slices among its threads according to its policy. This way no queue will be left behind. Reducing the time slice increases the number of context switches which can improve the threads' chances to progress at the expense of a larger total context switch overhead time.

We briefly discuss the distance-based and core affinity-based scheduling algorithm for the 2D mesh-connected AMC architecture of Fig. **1**. The scheduler maintains thread relevant information including: the thread's state, previous_CPU or core avoidance policies affinity which holds the core number on which the thread ran last, good_ fit which indicates if the core assignment is good (1) or can be improved (0), Thread Affinity (TA) which indicates the desire to be in proximity to the core hosting thread TA (ideally on the same core but on different logical processor), the thread's priority, and its class which reflects it core functionality and power requirements. Note that previous_CPU depends on the thread scheduling history, while TA may be intentionally specified by the programmer, or by the operating system.

Initially all queues are cleared and relevant structures are also cleared. The algorithm goes by each queue starting from highest to lowest priority and schedules each thread to its previous_CPU in order to satisfy core affinity if the previous_CPU assignment is a good fit (same class), or if the class to which previous_CPU belongs is not utilized by more than upc % (where upc is initialized to 75% and can be later changed by the operating system). If the previous_CPU is unavailable or belongs to a not-best-fit class with over 75% utilization, the thread may have to migrate to a core nearest (*i.e.* corresponding to a smaller inter-core distance as defined by equation 1 and Fig. **3**) to the previous_CPU in the same class, or if one is unavailable, to a core nearest to previous_CPU in the next higher class available. If no such cores are available in the same class or all higher classes, the thread is requeued in the same priority queued it was popped off thus implementing Round Robin policy within the same priority level.

When a core is assigned to the thread, a thread entry is queued into the cores' dispatch queue so that it can be executed. Note that priority inversion is avoided by scheduling first from higher priority queues.

SIMULATION FRAMEWORK AND RESULTS

In this section, we describe the simulator, present the simulation results, and compare the performance of the scheduling algorithm with various thread migration policies to other algorithms including one scheduling algorithm with various migration policies which was shown to be effective on SMT processors. For simplicity we assume that each core class has only multi- threaded cores, and that once a thread migrates to a new core, its good_fit is 1 or its CPU utilization is always lower than upc. In other words, the first choice of the scheduling algorithm is always the previous core, previous_CPU, on which the thread ran in the last quantum in which it was active. We also assume that the fairness policy never gets activated. For simplicity we ignore cache warming effects due to thread migration to another core. We consider and compare the following seven scheduling and/or migration algorithms.

    A.   a slight variation of the proposed affinity- and distance-based algorithm such that if the previous_CPU is not available then the scheduler looks to schedule the thread to cores in the vicinity of previous_CPU and if not possible, it schedules it on (*i.e.* migrates the thread to) the nearest available core in the next higher classes;

    B.   a scheduling algorithm with no concept of affinity which attempts to schedule the thread within its class if possible and then looks for the next higher class, following a sequential order of increasing core number starting with the lowest core number in the thread's previous_CPU 's class ; and

    C.   a non-migratory round robin scheduling algorithm [18, 26] that only attempts to reschedule an unfinished thread to the same previous_CPU core if available. Otherwise, it requeues the thread to the end of the priority queue.

    D.   A scheduling algorithm based on Prefer Last Move which was shown its effectiveness in ([29] by outperforming Symbiotic scheduling algorithms and other versions of Prefer Last, including Prefer Last Number, and Prefer Last Swap. In Prefer Last Move, a thread is picked randomly and is moved randomly to another core. The other threads are not moved but rescheduled to their Previous_CPU's. As our architecture is heterogeneous, we pick a thread randomly and migrate it to a random core with the desired functionality, so all cores in the thread's current class and upper classes participate in the core selection. The remaining threads remain scheduled on their existing cores until either they finish execution or they get picked in the next schedule iteration to move to another core as explained above. Algorithms D-G are exactly the same but differ in which thread is picked randomly to move to another core. In Algorithm D, we always pick a random thread from the priority 1 queue to move to another core at the start of scheduling iteration. If no other core is available, the randomly picked thread is not migrated. After scheduling all threads that can be scheduled in the 3 priority queues, another scheduling iteration is started and another randomly picked thread in the priority 1 queue is migrated to a randomly picked core with desired functionality.

    E.   Algorithm E is an exact copy of Algorithm D except here we randomly pick a thread from priority queue 2 to move to another core at the start of each scheduling iteration.

    F.   Algorithm F is an exact copy of Algorithm D except here we randomly pick a thread from priority queue 3 to move to another core at the start of each scheduling iteration.

    G.   Algorithm G is an exact copy of Algorithm D except here we randomly pick 3 threads, one for each of the 3 priority queues to move to another core at the start of each scheduling iteration.

Note that algorithms A, B and C are based on the proposed priority-based round robin scheduling algorithm but differ in their migration policies. We developed a simulator which integrates a model of the thread scheduling algorithms and their queue infrastructure in the C programming language and built, debugged, and validated in the Microsoft Visual.net Studio 2003 development environment. It is assumed that thread migration from a core to another core adjacent to it, referred to by 1 hop, takes 1 *cycle* to complete. Using this terminology, thread migration from core 8 to core 1 in Fig. **1** will take 4 hops or 4 cycles to complete. A time slice after which the operating system scheduler starts a new scheduling cycle is also assumed to consume 1 cycle. *It is important to remember that a cycle in this section does not refer to a CPU cycle but to one thread migration hop between neighboring cores or to one operating system time slice.* Therefore herein a cycle is equal to tens of CPU cycles. The simulator, whose skeleton is depicted in Fig. **4**, employs and defines some helper functions, including:

```
//Enter Selections
Set Affinity to           // 0 (if no core affinity is desired) or 1 (if affinity to previous_CPU is
desired)
Select hop duration; /*1 or 2 cycles */      Select Migration;      /* 1: if allowed */
Select XM; //0: nearest neighbor;1: assign 1st available core in list;
          //2: same as 1 but core is restricted to same class as thread
Define all_done1() //returns true when all threads in priority queue 1 are completed
Define all_done2() // returns true when all threads in priority queue 2 are completed
Define all_done3() // returns true when all threads in priority queue 3 are completed (
Define nocore(C)//returns T if no C class core is available (for all C class cores,
avail[C][cycle]=0)
Define get1core(CL, previous_CPU) which returns the core number assignment for a thread
which previously ran in previous_CPU --presently unavailable-- which belongs to class CL.
Get1core selects an available core in the same class CL, and if not available in another higher
class.
Define get2core(CL, previous_CPU) which returns the core number assignment for a thread
which previously ran in previous_CPU --presently unavailable-- which belongs to class CL.
Get2core selects an available core in the same class CL only.
Define get0core(CL, previous_CPU) which returns the core number assignment for a thread
which previously ran in previous_CPU --presently unavailable-- which belongs to class CL.
Get0core selects an available core in the same class CL, and if not available in another higher
class, according to nearest neighbor scheduling.
Define distance(a, b) which returns the number of hops between cores a and b
Main () {
Repeat 100 times
{Cycle=0; Randomly generate numbers of threads in each queue of the 3 priority queues; //0-
20
For each thread in each queue, randomly generate  its duration(1-3 cycles) &
previous_CPU(0-15);
Initialize all avail [core] [cycle] of all cores at all cycles to 0 (indicate cores are initially
available);
While (! alldone1() && alldone2() && alldone3()) //while still undone thread in queues 1-3
{cycle++;
If (! alldone1()) //while there are still uncompleted threads in queue 1
    {for each undone thread in queue 1
     { if affinity && previous_CPU is available
    {make core assigned to thread and set avail to occupied; decrement thread's duration;
         push thread to queue1's end;}
        else if migration is allowed
{switch (XM) //get new core assignment according to selected migration policy
              {0: get0core(); break; 1: get1core(); break;  2: get2core();}
        If another core C in a higher class is  available
        {calculate distance between C and previous_CPU;
     record that this new core C is unavailable;
         increment thread's penalty cycles by distance between C & previous_CPU ;
        set thread's previous_CPU to this core C;  decrement thread's duration;
        if duration is 0 log in output file the thread's completion time;
            push thread to end of queue 1; }
         }//if migration
    }//for each  undone thread
    }// if ! alldone1
If (! alldone2()) /* while there are still uncompleted threads in queue 2*/
{ …. // same as "If (! Alldone1())"but for queue 2}
If (! alldone3()) /* while there are still uncompleted threads in queue 3*/
{ …. // same as "If (! Alldone1())" but for queue 3}
} //while
 Update total penalty cycles with penalty cycles of all threads and total cycles with completion
cycles for this simulation run;
 }//Repeat
Print total and average penalty cycles and average cycles for all 100 simulation runs;}//Main
```

Figure 4: Pseudo-code of Thread Scheduling Simulator.

- all_done$i$(), where i is between 1 and 3, which returns true when all threads in priority queue i are completed, *i.e.* all threads in the ith priority queue have a duration of 0.;

- *nocore(C)* which returns *True* if no core is available in class C *i.e.* all cores in class C at current cycle have an avail of 0;

- *PushtoEnd(q, t)* which pushes thread t to end of queue q;

- *get1core(CL, previous_CPU)* which returns the core number assignment for a thread which previously ran in previous_CPU which is not currently available and therefore the thread cannot be reassigned to it, and where the desired core number belongs to class CL. Get1core selects an available core in the same class CL and if not available, in another higher class;

- *get2core(CL, previous_CPU)* which returns the core number assignment for a thread which previously ran in previous_CPU which is not currently available, and where the desired core number belongs to class CL. Get2core selects an available core in the same class CL only;

- *get0core(CL, previous_CPU)* which returns the core number assignment for a thread which previously ran in previous_CPU which is not currently available, and where the desired core number belongs to class CL. Get0core selects an available core in the same class CL and if not available in another higher class, according to the nearest neighbor scheduling algorithm;

- *distance(a, b)* returns the number of hops between cores a and b.

At the very start of the simulation, the selection is made as to whether core affinity and thread migrations are allowed, and if migration is permitted, a migration policy is selected. Also the time slice is set to either 1 cycle or 2 cycles (hops). Next, the following is repeated a hundred times, each time with a new simulation run with new queue contents. At the start of each of the 100 simulation runs, for each of the 3 priority queues, random number generating functions are called to generate

i. the number of threads in each queue (0-20);

ii. the duration of each thread, (1 or 2 cycles);

iii. the previous_CPU core number of the thread (0-15);

For each of the threads, two associated numbers are initialized to 0, *compt*, the completion time of the thread, and *penalty*, the penalty in cycles or hops incurred due to thread migration from the start of the simulation run at time 0 till the time when the thread fully completes execution. Simulation then proceeds as in Fig. 4 until all threads in all 3 priority queues finish execution, updating in each run the number of cycles it took for all the threads to complete execution and the total number of penalties (in hops or cycles) incurred by all migrating threads. Note that the total number of cycles, TNOC, represents the time (in cycles) of the last thread that completed its run and that the completion times of the other threads overlap with TNOC. However, the total number of penalties, TNOP, is accumulative and adds the penalties (in cycles) incurred by all threads. If a thread is not finished yet indicated by its duration having not yet reached 0, the thread is requeued at the end of the priority queue it belongs to after being processed, implementing Round Robin within the same priority level. Another simulation run is then started, with new number of threads in priority queues and their characteristics randomly generated and the procedure repeats until all 100 simulation runs each representing a different ensemble of threads' scenarios are completed. The final TNOC (TNOP) it took for all threads to complete after the 100th and final run, adds up all the TNOCs (TNOPs) from all 100 runs and is accumulative.

Table **1** shows the final TNOC and TNOP, the average TNOC per simulation run, the average TNOP per simulation run, and the final TNOC and TNOP normalized to the same values for algorithm A, for all 7 algorithms A-G. Among the 7 algorithms, algorithm A based on thread affinity and migration performs the best as it completes its total schedule in the fewest cycles. Algorithms B and C take 16.8% and 21.5% more cycles to finish the schedule. Algorithms D-G based on Prefer Last do much worse with at least 4.8x more cycles to complete. Algorithm A incurs a total of 5954 penalty cycles for migrating threads while algorithm B incurs and additional 11.08% penalty cycles as it does not use the concept of thread affinity but follows a blind schedule to the first available core in a sequence of cores. The TNOP for Algorithm C is 0 as this algorithm is non-migratory.

Table 1: Completion Times and Total Penalties for the Scheduling Algorithms

Algo-rithm	TNOC	TNOP	Avg NOC per simulation run	Avg NOP per simulation run	Avg TNOCs norma-lized to $TNOC_A$	Avg TNOPs norma-lized to $TNOP_A$
A	31776	5954	317.8	59.5	1	1
B	37120	65970	371.2	659.7	1.2	11.1
C	38592	0	385.2	0	1.2	0
D	172285	486894	1722.9	4868.9	5.4	81.8
E	168160	487493	1681.6	4874.9	5.3	81.9
F	152550	377661	1525.5	3776.6	4.8	63.4
G	240621	1203259	2406.2	12032.6	7.6	202.1

The penalties for the Prefer Last algorithms are much higher than the proposed algorithm explaining their poor performance. Migrating one randomly picked thread to a randomly picked location does not help performance in AMCs. The migration of the randomly picked thread helps increase the migration penalty cycles and keeping the other threads in place increases the wait times of the remaining unscheduled threads in the queue. Algorithm F performs better than E which performs better than D as the random thread in the lowest priority queue 3 that is migrated by Algorithm F gets migrated only after the schedulable threads in higher priority queues 1 and 2 have been allocated to cores, so certainly the migrated thread gets migrated to a core that does not delay the scheduling of higher priority threads.

It is clear from Table **1** that thread affinity and migration are helpful to the total schedule completion time, and that a scheme which allows thread migration but not thread affinity (algorithm B) outperforms a scheme which allows thread affinity but forbids thread migration (algorithm C).

When the thread duration is increased beyond 2 cycles, other simulation results (not presented in Table **1**) reveal that Algorithm A (as well as other variations of it which consider core affinity and allow thread migration to other cores if the previous core to which the thread was assigned to is unavailable but differ in which core to migrate the thread to in the latter case) outperform both non-affinity and non-migratory algorithms. However, as the thread duration increases, the difference in performance between Algorithm A and derivatives and non-affinity Algorithms B and derivatives shrank, in other words the relative performance of non-affinity algorithms improved with increasing thread duration. On the contrary, the performance of non-migratory algorithm C worsened with increasing thread duration. Non-migratory algorithm C outperformed non-affinity algorithms (such as B) when the maximum thread duration was between 3-30 cycles or time slices

Stressful workloads, higher resource contention and wait times increase the inter-core communication time. These result in longer hop durations or thread migration times. When the inter-core hop duration between 2 neighboring cores in the 2D mesh is doubled from 1 to 2 cycles, the completion times of non-affinity algorithms (such as B) increased significantly as each time when threads are re-scheduled, they are mapped to new cores incurring heavy moving penalties. The non-migratory algorithm (e. g. C) was affected the least as no thread hopping is allowed and therefore no migration penalties are incurred. (This is not to say that the non-migratory algorithm performs well as when no migration is allowed the thread must wait for longer times in a queue until the only core to which it can be assigned is available to host it again.) The distance-based and affinity based algorithm A's response time increase was moderate. The relative increase in completion time due to doubling the hop duration generally declined for algorithms A and derivatives (considering core affinity and allowing thread migration) as the maximum thread duration increased. This is because longer thread durations dilute the increases in hop duration and communication time. Therefore, increasing the hop duration is most detrimental to the non-Affinity algorithms which very likely incur migration costs on every thread re-scheduling, costs and penalties which become heftier with longer hop durations.

When threads are localized to a specific cores representing applications which are user(application) –constrained or system-constrained, algorithms such as A were found to perform best followed by non-affinity algorithms such as B.

Non-migratory algorithms performed the worst. The localized core affinity scenarios result in very long completion times of non-migratory algorithms as these cores are highly contended, while migratory algorithms relieve some of the pressure on these highly contended cores by migrating threads to other available cores.

RECONFIGURABILITY'S EFFECT ON SCHEDULING AND MIGRATION

Reconfiguration allows the system to transform itself to better suit the workload. By dynamically reconfiguring itself, the many-core system can result in a combination of better response time, power consumption, throughput, and/or availability. For instance, communication channels with lower latency or higher bandwidth could be enabled, more computing cores can be enabled to increase throughput or reduce response time or disabled to save on power consumption during periods of low activity. Also, access to faulty cores can be cut off and access to spare cores can be activated.

The reconfiguration of many-core CMPs and MPSoCs can take many forms. In one form, the core itself can go though a transformation to better suit the workload. The cores or components can be interconnected by various NoC topologies such as linear (bus), crossbar or mesh. For instance, the Reconfigurable Pipelined Datapath (RAPID) architecture [30] allows for the connections of components *via* bus connectors. The Programmable Arithmetic Device for DSP (PADDI) architecture [31], uses a crossbar switch to interconnect the various units. The MorphoSys architecture [32], uses a 2D Mesh interconnect. Other reconfigurable system are surveyed in [33]. Yet another type of reconfigurable systems reconfigures the core pipeline after the decode stage to suit the decoded instructions.

In another form, the interconnection network itself can be reconfigured to achieve different connections and permutations. Table **2** shows an example of such a network interconnecting 8 cores labeled 0-7. Various connections can be achieved by reconfiguring the network including 1-away (neighbor) exchange, right rotate, left rotate, shuffle, etc. In each table entry, each row corresponds to a different network configuration, and a new destination core number reached *via* this network is shown for each source core (top row). To reach all destinations, a message may have to make several passes over that network, possibly with the network configured differently in each pass. The network hardware itself implements these connections based on the desired configurations at a large hardware cost.

Table 2: Reconfigurable Network's Connections

Configuration	Core0	Core1	Core2	Core3	Core4	Core5	Core6	Core7
1-hop exchange	1	0	3	2	5	4	7	6
Right rotate	7	0	1	2	3	4	5	6
Left rotate	1	2	3	4	5	6	7	0
Shuffle	0	2	4	6	1	3	5	7
...								
2-hop exchange	2	3	0	1	6	7	4	5

In the era of many-core systems, network reconfiguration is done differently as each core is associated with a router as in Fig. **1**. With packet switching, the message is broken down into packets with each packet containing a destination address, and the network is simply reconfigured by changing the content of the routers' tables, and the router directs packets to specific router output ports as dictated by its routing table. Thus bypassing congested links or faulty ones and traffic redirection can be simply done by changing entry values in the routing table. In this approach, reconfiguration is simplified but end-to-end delays are not minimized as new routes do not necessarily go over direct links to the destination and may have to pass (and wait) in several routers before reaching the destination. Virtual channels –mapped to a single physical channel-- are used in modern wormhole routers to allow other traffic to use a physical channel, which another packet left unused because of blocking. [34] proposed a dynamically reconfigurable NoC which can add or remove express links between SoC elements by writing routing tables. Reconfiguration of routing tables consumes only 2 clock cycles or $0.02\mu s$ at 100MHz.

We now address the implications of system and NoC reconfiguration on the scheduling and migration of threads. In many-core systems employing a reconfigurable NoC, an application can be statically partitioned and compiled. At run time, dynamic mapping (to IP cores) and scheduling take place before the application executes. According to the static-time application partitioning and compilation, it may be desired to redefine the core classes of the AMC architecture to suit the workload. For instance, core classes may be dynamically redefined to include not cores of similar functionality but cores of different capabilities. Specifically, identical classes can be defined each one containing one GPU core and one DSP processor. Alternatively, classes can be redefined to vary in size and include a different number of IP cores as shown in Fig. **5**. As a result the new core migration priorities differ from the priorities of Fig. **3**. For instance in Fig. **5**, a thread previously assigned to core 0 in class B may prefer to be reassigned later to the same core if available (1st priority), or if unavailable to cores 2 or 4 in 2nd preference, or to core 6 as a third preference, and to cores in other classes if their functionality and availability permits and with priorities –or preferences—according to the core's distance to core 0 (previous_CPU). Hence various classes of cores can be formed to fit the workload.

The implications of class redefinitions on the scheduling and migration is that now given that the cores have been redistributed to new classes and selections of cores for migration have been reprioritized, scheduling algorithms A, B, and C are affected.

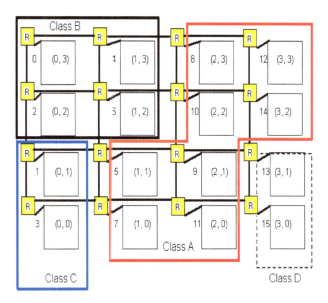

Figure 5: New class assignments after reconfiguration.

Migration-permitting algorithms A and B are affected as the selection of a new core for migration is altered as a result of changes in core priorities. Non-migratory algorithm C is also affected (as well as algorithms A and B) because the demand for (and availability of) previous_CPU may change (to the better or the worse) as a result of reconfiguration and class redefinitions and based on the workload's demands.

As a result of changes in link utilization and/or operability, it may be desired to dynamically reroute traffic though other communication paths to bypass congested or faulty paths. In that case, the classes may not need redefinition but the NoC's routing tables may need to be rewritten. The net effect is that the distance(a, b) in number of hops between cores a and b is modified to account for the new route between a and b. Plain Manhattan-style distances are substituted by the paths dictated by the new contents of the routing tables in the NoC's routers. As the distances in hops between pairs of cores are changed, the selection priorities of cores to which thread should migration also change as the priorities are based on the inter-distance between pairs of cores.

Therefore, in either case, whether dynamic system and/or NoC reconfiguration results in new class redefinitions or in rewriting of routing tables in the AMC architecture, distance- and class-based scheduling algorithms are affected.

The reconfigurability of the system and the NoC is not generally expected to change the performance of the scheduling algorithms. Algorithm A which attempts to reschedule the thread on the previous core it ran or migrated to the nearest core (according to the new contents of the routing tables) should still outperform algorithms B (with no concept of affinity) and C. Algorithm C which only attempts to reschedule the thread to the same core where it ran last may outperform algorithms A and B in rare cases or moments where the wait time for the availability of the previous_CPU is shorter than migrating the core. When thread durations are medium to long, these situations are rare. Algorithm A should always outperform B as A always attempt to reschedule to previous_CPU before exploring migration and because the selection of cores for migration (core priorities) follows a shorter distance order in A and a fixed order in B which does not minimize inter-core distances. Therefore the total migration costs incurred by A are still expected to be lower than those of B under reconfigurability.

CONCLUSION

Herein, we presented a distance- and affinity-based thread scheduling algorithm and evaluated various thread migration policies for a reconfigurable 2D mesh-connected class-based asymmetric many-core AMC processor architecture with Manhattan-style routing. Given the performance/Watt benefits of asymmetric (aka heterogeneous) many-core processors over homogeneous (aka symmetric) ones, and the benefits of providing multiple class cores to fit the various performance, power, and functionality demands of modern workloads, a class-partitioned AMC architecture was proposed. We presented a priority-based scheduling algorithm which may be associated with various thread migration policies for this AMC architecture.

We also described a simulator which we developed as a test bed for thread scheduling algorithms and migration policy performance evaluation. The simulator allows the selection of scheduling and migration policies, and generates relevant performance-related statistics which help in the performance assessment and comparison of the various migration algorithms considered. Other workload parameters can be selected including the maximum thread duration, the thread's core affinity, the migration penalty cost or hop duration.

We evaluated the performance of this thread scheduling algorithm with other migration policies based on round robin scheduling and Prefer Last Move. Prefer Last Move were shown to be effective in SMT processors. Simulation results revealed that when the scheduling algorithm considers both core affinity and thread migration in its scheduling decisions, it outperforms by at least 15% similar scheduling algorithms which ignore thread affinity or which are non-migratory in nature, and by at least 4.8x Prefer Last Move algorithms (Devuyst et al, 2006) which do not prevent starvation and migrate one random thread to another randomly-picked core thereby increasing migration penalty cycles.

When the thread duration is increased, algorithms which consider core affinity and allow thread migration outperform non-affinity algorithms and non-migratory ones. Non-migratory algorithm outperformed non-affinity algorithms for maximum thread duration between 3-30 time slices. Relative to algorithms which consider core affinity and allow thread migration, non-affinity algorithms' relative performance improves with increased thread duration. Non-migratory algorithms' performance worsens relatively more as the thread duration is increased.

As the thread migration cost or hop duration is increased, non-affinity algorithms are most affected and their performance worsens significantly. The performance loss of algorithms which consider core affinity and allow thread migration were more moderate with performance losses evaporating with increasing thread durations.

Therefore it is essential for scheduling algorithms for asymmetric many-cores to be based on core affinities and to allow thread migration in case of previous core unavailability. We also evaluated our priority-based affinity-based migration-allowing scheduling algorithm with several migration policies, some assigning the destination core to which the thread should be migrated as: i. the nearest neighbor core starting from the same class as the previous_CPU onward to higher core classes; ii. a core in a list of cores strictly belonging to the same class as the previous core on which the thread ran previously; or iii. a core in a list of cores ordered from the same class as previous_CPU onward to higher core classes. Simulation results reveal that nearest-neighbor migration is best when the maximum thread duration was up to 9 times the hop duration. When the thread duration was larger than that, the specific migration policy did not matter much as long as the algorithm was affinity based and allowed thread migration.

This Chapter also addressed the implications of system and NoC reconfigurability on the perfor-mance of distance-based thread scheduling algorithms and migration policies. In the AMC architecture, reconfiguration could result in core class redefinitions and/or rewriting routing tables. It was discussed how this affected the various considered distance-based scheduling algorithms and migration policies in the NoC-based AMC architecture. It is worthy of investigating in the future if the ranking of the considered algorithms changes as a result of the reconfiguration of the number of classes and/or number of cores per class under general workloads based on extensive simulations.

REFERENCES

[1]   Jouppi N. The Future evolution of high-performance microprocessors. Keynote Speech. In Proc. Intl. Symposium on Microarchitecture; 2005: New York: ACM Press.

[2]   Kahle J *et al.* Introduction to the Cell multiprocessor. IBM J Res Develop 2005.

[3]   Kumar R, Tullsen D, and Jouppi N. Heterogeneous chip multiprocessors. IEEE Comput 2005: 32-38.

[4]   Sibai, FN. Dissecting the PCMark®05 benchmark and assessing performance scaling. In Proc. 3rd IEEE Int. Conference on Innovations in Information Technology; 2006: Dubai, UAE: IEEE Press.

[5]   Hammond L *et al.* A single-chip multiprocessor. IEEE Comput 1997;30(9)

[6]   Kalla R, *et al.* IBM POWER5 chip: A dual-core multithreaded processor. IEEE MICRO 2004

[7]   Kongetira P, *et al.* A 32-way multithreaded SPARC processor. IEEE Micro 2005

[8]   McNairy C, and Bhatia R. Montecito: a dual-core, dual-thread Itanium processor. IEEE MICRO 2005.

[9]   Constantinou T *et al.* Performance implications of single thread migration on a chip multi-core. ACM SIGARCH Computer Architecture News 2005; 33(4)

[10]   Shaw K, and Dally B. Migration in single chip multiprocessors. IEEE Comp. Arch. Letters 2002;1(3)

[11]   Avnur R *et al.* Thread migration in the River dataflow environment (Tech. Report). Berkeley: University of California, CS Dept. 2003

[12]   Hily S and Seznec A. Contention on 2nd level cache may limit the effectiveness of simultaneous multithreading (Report # 1086). IRISA INRIA 1997

[13]   Balakrishnan S, Rajwar R, Upton M, and Lai K. The impact of performance asymmetry in emerging multicore architectures. In Proc. 32nd Int. Symposium on Computer Architecture; 2005: New York: ACM Press.

[14]   Kim S *et al.* Fair cache sharing and partitioning in a chip multiprocessor architecture. In Proc. of the 13th IEEE Conf. on Parallel Architecture and Compilation techniques; 2004: Piscataway: IEEE Press.

[15]   Chandra D *et al.* Predicting inter-thread cache contention on a chip multi-processor architecture. In Proc. 11th IEEE Symp. on High-Performance Computer Architecture (HPCA-11); 2005: Piscataway: IEEE Press.

[16]   Fedorova A *et al. Cache-fair thread scheduling for multicore processors* (Tech. Report TR-17-06). Cambridge: Harvard University, Engineering and Applied Sciences 2006

[17]   Fedorova A. *Operating system scheduling for chip multithreaded processors.* Unpublished doctoral dissertation, Cambridge, MA: Harvard University 2006

[18]   Silberschatz A *et al. Operating Systems Concepts*. NY: John Wiley and Sons 2004

[19]   Chapin S. Distributed and multiprocessor scheduling. ACM Computing Surveys 1996 ; 28(1).

[20]   Chandra R *et al.* Scheduling and page migration for multiprocessor compute servers. In Proc. 6th Conf. on Arch. Support for Prog. Languages and Operating Systems; 1994: New York: ACM Press.

[21]   Squillante M, Lazowska E. Using processor-cache affinity in shared-memory multiprocessor scheduling. IEEE Trans. on Parallel & Distributed Systems 1993; 4(2)

[22]   Torrellas J, Tucker A, and Gupta A. Evaluating the benefits of cache-affinity scheduling in shared-memory multiprocessors. Proc SIGMETRICS; 1993: NY: ACM,

[23]   Vaswani R *et al.* The implications of cache affinity on processor scheduling for multiprogrammed, shared memory multiprocessors. In Proc. ACM Symp.OS Principles; 1991: New York: ACM Press.

[24]   Osterhout J. Scheduling techniques for concurrent systems. In Proc. 3rd Int Conf. on Distributed Comp. Systems; 1982: Piscataway: IEEE Press.

[25]   Arora N *et al.* Thread scheduling for multiprogrammed multiprocessors. In Proc. ACM SPAA; 1998: New York: ACM Press.

[26]   Parekh S, Eggers S, Levy H, and Lo J. Thread-sensitive scheduling for SMT processors (Tech. report 2000-04-02). Seattle, USA: Univ. of Washington 2000

[27]   Bulpin J, Pratt I. Hyper-threading aware process scheduling heuristics. In *Proc. USENIX Technical Conference;* 2005: New York: ACM Press.

[28]   Snavely A, Tullsen D. Symbiotic job scheduling for a simultaneous multithreading processor. In Proc. 9th ACM International Conference on Architectural Support for Programming Languages and Operating Systems (ASPLOS'00); 2000: New York: ACM Press.

[29]   DeVuyst M *et al.* Exploiting unbalanced thread scheduling for energy and performance on a CMP of SMT processors. In Proc. 20th IEEE Int. Parallel and Distrib. Proc. Symp.; 2006: Piscataway: IEEE Press.

[30]   Ebeling C, Cronquist D, and Franklin P. RaPiD - Reconfigurable Pipelined Datapath. In Proc. 6th International Workshop on Field-Programmable Logic and Applications; 1996.

[31]   Chen D. Programmable Arithmetic Devices for High Speed Digital Signal Processing. (Technical Report No. UCB/ERL M92/49). Berkeley: University of California, EECS Department 1992.

[32]   Lee M *et al.* Design and Implementation of the MorphoSys Reconfigurable Computing Processor. J VLSI Signal Process Sys 2000; 24 (2-3): 147-164.

[33]   Compton K, Hauck S. Reconfigurable Computing: A Survey of Systems and Software. ACM Computing Surveys 2002; 34 (2): 171–210

[34]   Rana V, Atienza D, Santambrogio M, Sciuto D, and De Micheli G. A Reconfigurable Network-on-Chip Architecture for Optimal Multi-Processor SoC Communication, VLSI-SoC (2008).

[35]   Kavaldjiev NK. A run-time reconfigurable Network-on-Chip for streaming DSP applications. PhD thesis, Netherlands: University of Twente. CTIT Ph.D.-thesis series No. 06-91 ISBN 90-365-2410-5 2007.

[36]   Abdel-Shafi H *et al.* Efficient user-level checkpoint-ting and thread migration in Windows NT clusters. Proc. 3rd Usenix Windows Symp.; 1999: Seattle: ACM.

CHAPTER 2

On the Design of Multicore Architectures Guided by a Miss Table at Level-1 and Level-2 Caches to Improve Predictability and Performance/Power Ratio

Abu Asaduzzaman* and Fadi N. Sibai

Department of Computer and Electrical Engineering and Computer Science, Florida Atlantic University, Boca Raton, Florida 33431, USA

Abstract: Most contemporary architectures for high-performance low-power computing systems consist of multicore processors, where tasks are distributed among multiple cores to improve processing speed and the system runs at a lower frequency to reduce the total power consumption. However, multilevel caches in multicore architectures multiply the timing unpredictability and require significant amount of power to be operated. Cache locking techniques are used in single-core systems to improve predictability by locking useful blocks in the cache. The success of cache locking primarily depends on the effective selection of the right blocks to be locked. In prior work, we introduced an efficient block selection methodology and a Miss Table based cache locking scheme where information about the blocks and cache misses are stored in the Miss Table to facilitate the cache locking. Cache locking in multicore is more challenging because of the complexity introduced by the architecture. In this chapter, we investigate the impact of the particular placement of the Miss Table, *i.e.* whether at the level-1 cache (CL1) or at level-2 cache (CL2), on the system's predictability and performance/power ratio. Using VisualSim and Heptane simulation tools, we simulate an 8-core architecture, where each core's private CL1 is split into instruction (I1) and data (D1) caches and the CL2 is unified and shared by the cores. Experimental results using MPEG4 decoding and FFT algorithms show that Miss Table based cache locking at level-1 is more beneficiary than Miss Table based cache locking at level-2 for MPEG4; a maximum reduction of 38% in mean delay per task and a maximum reduction of 32% in total power consumption are achieved by locking one-fourth of the I1 cache size. For FFT, the impact of locking at level-1 and level-2 is almost the same.

INTRODUCTION

Single-core processors are no longer adequate for supporting high-performance computing. The algorithms for high-performance real-time computing are more complicated than those currently being used. For example, real-time multimedia computing uses a visual paradigm rather than a conventional text paradigm and deals with large image files including video sequences. In addition to performance, power consumption is an important design factor and power consumption/dissipation should be kept as minimum as possible. Also, execution time predictability is crucial to support real-time applications. According to the newly emerged multicore design, two cores running at one half of the frequency can approach the performance of a single core running at full frequency, while the dual core consumes significantly less amount of power. Because of their high performance/power ratio, the multicore processors open new possibilities for system designers in implementing highly complex multimedia computing algorithms as described by Suhendra *et al.* [1]. In a multicore architecture, two or more independent cores are combined into a die. In most cases, each processor has its own private level-1 cache memory (CL1). Normally, the CL1 is split into instruction (I1) and data (D1) caches. Also, multicore processors may have one shared level-2 cache (CL2) or multiple distributed and dedicated CL2s. Asaduzzaman *et al.* [2] shows that cache parameters (such as cache size, line size, and associativity levels) significantly influence system performance. Multicore architectures are more suitable for high-performance real-time applications, because concurrent execution of tasks on a single processor is inadequate for achieving the required level of performance and reliability. The integration of billions of transistors in a single chip is now possible. As a result, the multicore design trend is expected to grow for the next decade. Multicore architecture has multiple levels of caches. Cache requires additional power to be operated and introduces timing unpredictability. Even though cache improves performance by bridging the speed between the main memory and CPU, the presence of caches makes the multicore system more power hungry and unpredictable. Therefore, it becomes a great challenge to design and implement cache memory subsystem in multicore architectures. A better use of the cache memory subsystem can be very effective to improve the predictability and performance/power ratio.

*Address correspondence to Dr. Abu Asaduzzaman: Department of Computer and Electrical Engineering and Computer Science, Florida Atlantic University, Boca Raton, Florida 33431, USA; Tel: +1-561-297-2452; E-mail: aasaduzz@fau.edu

Pao-Ann Hsiung, Yean-Ru Chen and Chao-Sheng Lin (Eds)

Cache locking shows promises to improve predictability as shown by [3-8]. Cache locking can be effectively used to improve performance/power ratio [3]. Cache locking is defined as the ability to put off some or all of the data or instruction cache from being overwritten. Cache entries can be locked either for individual ways within the cache or for the entire cache. In way locking, only a portion of the cache is locked by locking ways within the cache. Unlocked ways of the cache behave normally. Harrison [9] and Stokes [10] show that way locking improves the predictability and performance. Using way locking, the Intel Xeon processor achieves the effect of using local storage by the Synergistic Processing Elements (SPEs) in the IBM Cell processor architecture. In entire cache locking, cache hits are treated in the same manner as hits to an unlocked cache. Cache misses are treated as a cache-inhibited access. Invalid cache entries at the time of the locking will remain invalid and inaccessible until the cache is unlocked. Entire cache locking is inefficient when the size of the data or the number of the instructions to be locked is smaller compared to the cache size.

In currently available single-core way cache locking techniques, the blocks to be locked are selected by off-line analysis of the applications. The information collected by off-line analysis, can be post-processed and re-used in single-core and/or multicore systems to facilitate the efficient selection of blocks to be pre-loaded and locked and/or selection of victim block to be replaced. An efficient block selection methodology is previously introduced, which depends on the number of cache misses by each block. Miss Table-based cache locking scheme is also introduced where information about the blocks and the cache misses are stored in the Miss Table to facilitate the cache locking. In this Chapter, we investigate the impact of Miss Table based cache locking at level-1 and Miss Table-based cache locking at level-2 on the predictability and performance/power ratio. We model an 8-core architecture, where each CL1 is split into I1 and D1 and unified CL2 is shared by the cores. We use workloads from MPEG4 decoding and FFT algorithms to run the simulations.

This Chapter is organized as follows. In Section 2, some related literature is discussed. Multicore architectures with Miss Tables are introduced in Section 3. In Section 4, simulation details and some important results are presented. This Chapter is concluded in Section 5. Finally, VisualSim Block Diagram and VisualSim Simulation Cockpit of an 8-core architecture are shown in appendices A and B.

LITERATURE SURVEY

Power-aware high-performance computing architecture for real-time systems has become an important research topic in the recent years. A lot of work has been done to improve predictability and performance/ power ratio in single-core systems by cache locking. In this section, we first briefly discuss some cache memory hierarchy, followed by various existing single-core cache locking techniques. Then, we present a number of cache memory hierarchies used in contemporary popular multicore processors. In the next section, we focus on 2 similar selected multicore architectures, one with Miss Tables at level-1 caches and the other one with Miss Table at level-2 cache.

Cache memory has a very rich history in the evolution of modern computing as summarized in Smart Cache [11]. Cache memory is first seen in the IBM System/360 Model 85 in late 1960s. In 1989, Intel 468DX microprocessor introduced on-chip 8 KB CL1 cache for the first time. In early 1990s, off-chip CL2 cache appeared with 486DX4 and Pentium microprocessor chips. Today's microprocessors usually have 128 KB or more of CL1, and 512 KB or more of CL2, and optional 2 MB or more CL3. Romanchenko [12] mentions some CL1 cache is split into I1 and D1 in order to improve performance. Torres [13] discusses Intel Pentium 4 processor, one of the most popular single-core processors that use inclusive cache architecture. A typical inclusive cache is shown in Fig. **1**. CL2 contains each and every blocks that CL1 (*i.e.*, I1 and D1) may contain. In case of a CL1 miss followed by a CL2 miss, the block is first brought into CL2 from main memory, then into CL1 from CL2. Intel Pentium 4 Willamette is a single-core processor that has on-die 256 KB inclusive level-2 cache; with 8 KB level-1 trace/instruction cache (I1) and 8 KB level-1 data cache (D1).

Vera *et al.* [14] propose a memory hierarchy with dynamic locking cache is proposed to provide high performance combined with high predictability for complex systems. They conclude in an intuitive way that faster execution times are possible. However, it is very difficult to provide the necessary locking information into the program code since both the hardware and the software might be involved. Arnaud *et al.* [15] introduces a methodology using genetic algorithm that can be used to select a set of instructions to be preloaded and locked in the cache. This scheme may improve predictability by selecting the target set of instructions efficiently. However, the algorithm used in this scheme can be also misleading, because it uses neither the information about task structure nor the problem parameters. Tamura *et al.* [16] studies the impact of three different fitness functions. These fitness functions are used in a genetic algorithm that selects the contents of a static locking cache memory in a real-time system. Results indicate that none of the fitness functions perform well in the two basic metrics used. Tamura *et al.* [8] combines static cache analysis with data cache locking to estimate the worst-case memory performance in a safe, tight and fast way. Experimental results show that this scheme is more predictable. However, a better analysis that classifies the cache accesses as misses or hits and locks fewer regions could be beneficial. [17] proposes a dynamic cache locking algorithm which partitions the task into a set of regions. Each region owns statically a locked cache content determined offline. A sharp improvement is observed, as compared with a system without caches. However, this technique is not capable of power estimation – a crucial design factor for embedded systems. Above mentioned techniques are developed to evaluate predictability in a single-core system and they are not adequate to analyze performance, power consumption, and predictability of multicore real-time systems.

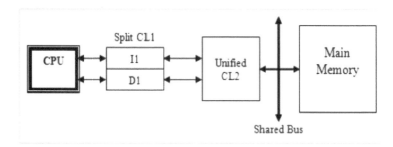

Figure 1: Inclusive cache architecture.

Most manufacturers are adopting multicore processors to acquire required high processing power for the future multimedia computing systems. Popular multicore processors from Intel, AMD, and IBM have multilevel caches as discussed in Romanchenko [18], Multicore [19], and Every [20]. As shown in Fig. **2**, Intel quad-core Xeon DP has 128 KB I1, 128 KB D1, and 8 MB shared CL2.

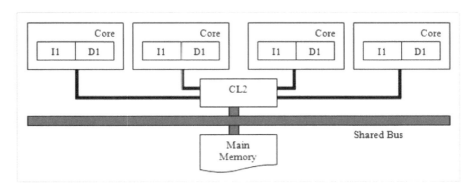

Figure 2: Intel quad-core Xeon DP architecture.

AMD quad-core Opteron has 256 KB I1, 256 KB D1, 2 MB distributed and dedicated CL2 and 2 MB (Santa Rosa) or 4 MB (Deerhound) shared CL3.

Sibai [21] studies various shared and distributed and dedicated cache memory organizations and the impact of sharing and privatizing them on performance in homogeneous multicore architectures.

IBM's Cell multicore processor has a Primary Processing Entity (PPE) like IBM dual-threaded PowerPC and 8 Cells. Stokes [22], Blachford [23], and Vance [24] summarize Cell-like multicore architecture (see Fig. **3**). Each Cell is also called a Synergistic Processing Elements (SPE). The PPE contains a 32 KB I1 and a 32 KB D1 caches. A 512 KB CL2 is shared by the PPE and SPEs. Primarily the PowerPC PPE keeps the processor compatible with lots of applications. Each SPE has 256 KB SRAM and a 4 x 128 bit ALU (Arithmetic Logical Unit which does the math in a processor), and 128 of 128-bit registers. The Element Interconnect Bus (EIB) is the communication bus internal to the Cell processor which connects the various on-chip system elements: PPE processor, memory controller (MIC), eight SPE coprocessors, and two off-chip I/O interfaces.

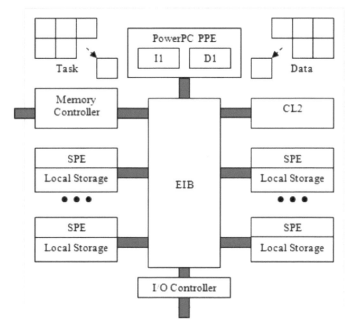

Figure 3: IBM Cell-like multicore architecture.

MULTICORE ARCHITECTURE and MISS TABLES

We have discussed the cache memory hierarchy in some popular single-core and multicore processors and some existing cache locking techniques. In this section, we discuss Miss Table in multicore architectures. Miss Table is populated with information of blocks which cause cache misses (without cache locking) by post-processing the results of worst case execution time (WCET) analysis of the applications. The main goal of introducing MT is improving cache locking performance. The presence of the MT opens an opportunity for the cache locking scheme to lock blocks from the top of the MT (those with most misses) – that increases cache hit and predictability and decreases total power consumption. In addition, the contents of the MT can guide the pre-loading and replacement strategies. During pre-loading CL1, those blocks should be loaded first (using MT) which are identified to create more misses. The cache replacement strategy should select a block with minimum number of misses using MT. Thus the contents of the MT can guide the pre-loading and replacement strategies. Cache locking guarantees a cache hit of the locked block while not replacing the block and extending the block's hit rate. As a block hits in the cache, predictability improves consistently as no additional steps are required to locate and fetch the addressed item from higher and slower levels of the memory hierarchy. As a result, the architecture (with MT) makes better usage of the caches using the MT and should significantly improve the predictability and performance/power ratio. In the following subsections, we discuss the architectures with MT, Miss Table, cache replacement policy, main memory update policy, and multicore cache locking algorithm.

Multicore Architectures

Multicore architectures are complex with multiple levels of cache memories. Miss Table(s) can be implemented at level-1 caches or at level-2 cache. Figs. **4a** and **4b** illustrate the multicore architectures with 8 cores. As shown in Fig. **4a**, at first, MT is considered at level-2 cache; CL1s can access the MT. Then, MTs are considered at level-1 caches as shown in Fig. **4b**. Along with MT, each core has one private CL1 which is split into I1 and D1 for improved performance. We select Intel-like shared CL2 multicore architecture in our experiments. The unified CL2 may be partitioned into parts to reduce bus contention so that only a few cores can access each part. Cache locking is implemented in I1 when the MT is at level-1 cache and cache locking is implemented in CL2 when the MT is at level-2 cache.

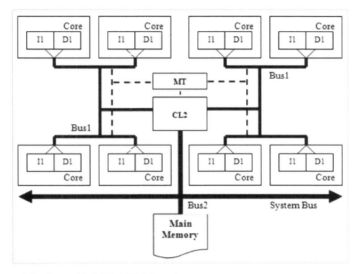

Figure 4a: Simulated 8-core architecture with MT at CL2 Level.

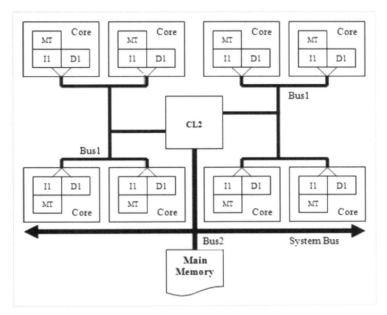

Figure 4b: Simulated 8-core architecture with MT at I1 Level.

Miss Table

A Miss Table (MT) is a table that contains the information about all or top-most blocks that cause cache misses (if not locked) – information includes block addresses and number of misses and are sorted in descending order of the number of misses.

For each application (or code segment), after post-processing the tree-graph generated by Heptane, data (containing the block address and total number of misses) is prepared for the MT. The MT can be implemented at any level of caches (CL1 or CL2). MT-based cache locking scheme would pick the top entries of the MT (with the maximum number of misses) to be locked. This will ensure that the locked blocks with most misses will not be replaced thereby prolonging their stay in the cache and enhancing their future hit rates. Similarly, an efficient pre-loading technique using the MT would select the top entries of the MT (with the maximum number of misses) to be pre-loaded. However, a modified/efficient cache replacement policy using the MT would pick the bottom entry of the MT (with the least number of misses) to be replaced.

MT not only improves cache locking performance, it may improve the performance of cache replacement and pre-loading scheme. Therefore, MT may improve the predictability and performance/ power ratio.

Cache Replacement Policy

A modified (and better) cache replacement policy is adopted (for I1 and CL2 instructions) in this Chapter. When the cache is full and a new block needs to be brought into the cache, using MT information, this policy always selects an unlocked instruction block with the minimum number of misses as the victim block that should be replaced by the new block. In case of a tie in the number of misses, a block is selected randomly. Random cache replacement policy is used for D1 and CL2 data.

Memory Update Policy

In this Chapter, write through memory update is considered to facilitate cache locking (at I1 or at CL2) and to avoid any cache inconsistency. Thus, if a write occurs at the I1 level, the locked copy (whether it is in I1 or CL2) is updated along with the main memory copy.

Multicore Cache Locking Algorithm

In this subsection, we briefly discuss the algorithm of cache locking technique at level-1 cache (*i.e.*, I1) and level-2 cache (*i.e.*, CL2) in a multicore architecture. We assume the multicore architecture be a homogeneous one where all cores are similar. Each core has the same size I1 and D1 and can perform the same tasks. According to this algorithm, incoming tasks (*i.e.*, requests) come to the controller of the multicore. The controller assigns the incoming task to a free core (if any) and marks the core as busy. If no free core is found, incoming tasks are put into a waiting queue and served when cores become available (*i.e.*, free) in a first come first serve basis.

In case of I1 cache locking, depending on the assigned task to a core, the respective MT is populated, the pre-selected blocks are loaded, and a portion of the cache (I1 in this case) is locked. Then the core starts processing the task. In case of a cache miss when cache is already full, it selects the victim block (an un-locked block with the minimum number of misses) using the MT and modified cache replacement policy. When the task is finished, the MT is made clear. The core is made free (*i.e.*, available).

In case of CL2 cache locking, MT is populated at the start-up, the pre-selected blocks are loaded, and a portion of the cache (CL2 in this case) is locked. The MT information is used by I1 and CL2 to select the victim blocks for cache replacement.

SIMULATION

We develop a simulation platform to investigate the impact of Miss Table based cache locking at level-1 caches and Miss Table-based cache locking at level-2 cache on predictability and performance/power ratio. We use Heptane simulation package to generate workload using MPEG4 decoding and FFT algorithms to run the simulation program. We use VisualSim simulation tool to develop the model, to execute the simulation, and to collect results. First, we briefly present the simulation details. Then, we discuss some important simulation results.

Simulation Details

We model a multicore architecture with 8 processing cores and 2-level cache memory subsystem. We simulate Miss Table-based cache locking at level-1 caches and Miss Table-based cache locking at level-2 cache using Moving Picture Experts Group's MPEG4 (part-2) decoding and Fast Fourier Transform (FFT) workloads. The code size for MPEG4 and FFT are 29,937 Bytes and 2,335 Bytes, respectively. These applications were selected due to their popularity and to their code differences and signatures (for instance, the code sizes are very different, one easily fitting inside the CL1 while the other does not). We generate a tree-graph for each application code that shows the blocks that cause misses and the number of misses by single-core WCET analysis. By post-processing the tree-graph, we create an MT for each application. MT information is used to select the right blocks for cache locking and the victim blocks for cache replacement. In this subsection, we briefly discuss some assumptions, simulation tools, and important input and output parameters.

Assumptions

We make the following important assumptions,

- Way cache locking is implemented in this work; 25% of I1 and CL2 cache size is locked for optimal performance.

- A modified cache replacement strategy is used for I1 and CL2 that selects the victim blocks using MT information.

- Write-through memory update policy is used.

- The delay introduced by the bus that connects CL2 and the main memory (Bus2 in Figs. **4a** and **4b**) is 15 times longer than the delay introduced by the bus that connects CL1 and CL2 (Bus1 in Figs. **4a** and **4b**).

- The cache hit ratio is adjusted/increased when the cache size, line size, or associativity is increased.

- The changes in cache hit/miss times due to the increase in cache size, line size, and associativity are assumed to be negligible compared to the obtained reduction in mean delay per task.

- We simulate a multicore system with 8 cores and MT(s). However, because of Heptane and VisualSim simulator limitations, the workload we use are single-threaded and our simulation simulates one application running on one core at a time. The other cores are idle at that time. Thus no multiple cache effects are simulated.

- Because of Heptane limitation, only misses in the I1 are captured. Thus locking experiments only apply to the instruction blocks.

Simulation Tools

VisualSim and Heptane simulation tools are used in this work. VisualSim (a.k.a., VisualSim Architect) from Mirabilis Design is a graphical system-level simulation tool VisualSim [25]. We install VisualSim in Windows XP in a Dell PowerEdge 1600SC PC. Using VisualSim, we model the abstracted architecture. Using VisualSim simulation cockpit, we run the simulation program and obtain simulation results. The results are stored as text and/or graph files.

Heptane (Hades Embedded Processor Timing ANalyzEr) is a WCET analysis tool for embedded systems Heptane [26]. Prior to running simulations on VisualSim, we configure Heptane in Red Hat Linux 9 in the same Dell PowerEdge 1600SC PC (where we have VisualSim in Windows XP). Once the configuration file is created, Heptane is run by typing "heptane-run.sh'" in a command shell provided that the PATH variable contains the directory where Heptane is installed. The results are placed in the directory as specified in the configuration file and are viewed through a Web browser by opening the file "HTML/index.html". A limitation of Heptane is that it only gives instruction miss information but no data miss information.

Input and Output Parameters

Important input parameters are shown in Table **1**. We simulate an 8-core system with I1, D1, and CL2. We keep CL2 size fixed at 128 KB and vary the I1/D1 size, CL1/CL2 line size and associativity level.

Table 1: Important Input Parameters

Parameter	Value
Number of cores	8 (fixed)
I1 (/D1) cache size (KB)	2, 4, 8, 16, or 32
CL2 cache size (KB)	64, 128, 256, 512, or 1024
CL1/CL2 line size (Byte)	16, 32, 64, 128, or 256
CL1/CL2 associativity level	1-, 2-, 4-, 8-, or 16-way

Output parameters include average delay per task (to represent the performance) and total power consumption.

Results

In this work, we model an 8-core architecture and simulate Miss Table based cache locking at I1 and Miss Table based cache locking at CL2 to study the impact on the predictability and performance/power ratio for multicore systems. We run the simulation program using MPEG4 decoding and FFT workloads. We obtain results by varying the I1/CL2 cache size, CL1/CL2 line size, and CL1/CL2) associativity level with and without applying Miss Table based cache locking at I1 and CL2. Based on prior work [2, 27], we apply 25% cache locking in this work for the optimal performance. In the following subsections, we discuss the impact of I1/CL2 cache size, CL1/CL2 line size, and CL1/CL2 associativity level on average delay per task and total power consumption.

I1/CL2 Cache Size

We obtain the average delay per task for various I1(/D1)/CL2 cache size for no locking and 25% cache locking at I1 (MT is at level-1 cache) and CL2 (MT is at level-2 cache) using MPEG4 decoding and FFT workloads. Simulation results are shown in Fig. **5**. Here, "MPEG4 L2/No-Lock" means simulation is run using MPEG4 decoding workload when MT is at level-2 cache and cache locking is not applied (but victim blocks are selected using MT information for cache replacement). Also, "MPEG4 L2/Lock" means simulation is run using MPEG4 decoding workload when MT is at level-2 cache and cache locking is applied (and victim blocks are selected using MT information for cache replacement). Simulation results show that for any I1/CL2 cache size used, the mean delay per task for MPEG4 decoding workload decreases when MT-based cache locking is applied at I1 (MT is at level-1 cache). As expected, results show that average delay per task decreases with the increase in I1/CL2 cache size for MPEG4. For FFT, average delay per task decreases at the beginning (2/64 KB to 4/128 KB), after that delay remains almost the same. This is because the FFT code fits entirely in I1 for I1 cache size is equal to 4KB or higher.

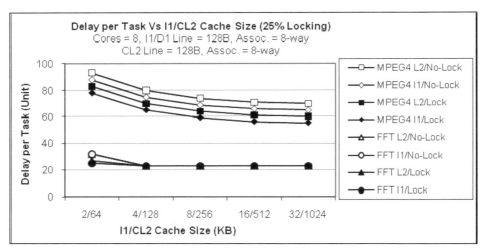

Figure 5: Mean delay per task versus cache size (MT at I1/CL2).

Cache is power hungry. The impact of MT-based cache locking at I1 (MT is at level-1 cache) and MT-based cache locking at CL2 (MT is at level-2 cache) on total power consumption is shown in Fig. **6**. Simulation results show that for MPEG4, total power consumption decreases when MT-based cache locking is applied at I1 (MT is at level-1 cache) for any I1/CL2 cache size used. Results also show that total power consumption decreases with the increase in I1/CL2 cache size for MPEG4 workload. For FFT, even though total power consumption decreases at the beginning (2/64 KB to 4/128 KB), it starts increasing with the increase of I1/CL2 size from 4/128 KB. This is because small FFT code does not take advantage of higher cache size (and MT-based cache locking).

I1/CL2 Line Size

We use the same line size for I1, D1, and CL2. Fig. **7** shows the average delay per task versus I1/CL2 line size for no locking and 25% I1 and CL2 cache locking. It is observed that the average delay per task goes down for MPEG4, but not for FFT, with increasing line size leveling off at 128B. For line size greater than 128B, the average delay per task increases for MPEG4 due to the cache pollution and remains the same for FFT.

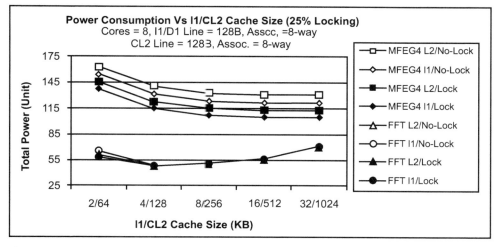

Figure 6: Total power consumption versus cache size (MT at I1/CL2).

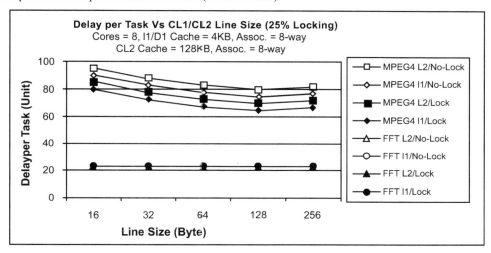

Figure 7: Mean delay per task versus line size (MT at I1/CL2).

Similarly, total power consumption decreases for MPEG4, but not for FFT, with increasing line size leveling off at a line size of 128B (see Fig. **8**). It is observed that for line size greater than 128B, the total power consumption increases for MPEG4 and remains the same for FFT.

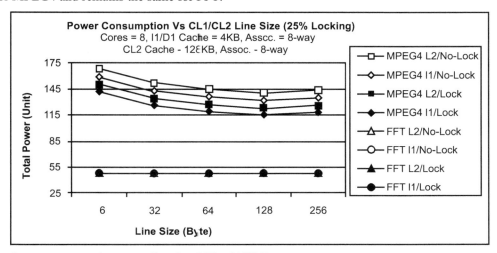

Figure 8: Total power consumption versus line size (MT at I1/CL2).

I1/CL2 Associativity Level

In this experiment, the associativity level is kept the same for I1, D1, and CL2. The impact of MT-based cache locking (25% of cache size) at level-1 and level-2 cache on the mean delay per task and total power consumption is illustrated in Figs. **9** and **10** by varying the associativity level. Experimental results show that for any associativity level (from 1-way to 16-way), the mean delay per task for MPEG4 decreases when we move from no locking to I1/CL2 locking (see Fig. **9**). The decrease in the mean delay per task is significant for smaller levels of associativity (1-way to 2-way), after 4-way the mean delay per task remains almost the same. For I1 size of 4KB (or higher), MT-based cache locking and the associativity level has no positive impact on FFT.

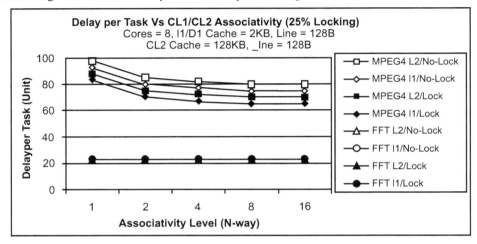

Figure 9: Mean delay per task versus associativity level (MT at I1/CL2).

Fig. **10** shows the impact of MT-based cache locking (25% of cache size) at level-1 and level-2 cache on total power consumption for various associativity levels. For associativity level from 1-way to 16-way, the total power consumption due to MPEG4 decreases when MT-based I1/CL2 cache locking is used. However, the decrease in total power consumption is significant between 1-way and 4-way. For FFT, the total power consumption remains almost the same.

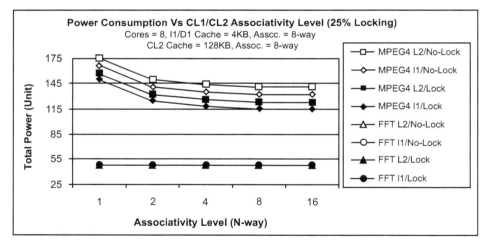

Figure 10: Total power consumption versus assoc. level (MT at I1/CL2).

Finally, we summarize the changes in mean delay and total power consumption. The decrement is represented with a leading (-) and the increment is represented with a leading (+). As shown in Table **2**, both the mean delay per task and total power consumption decreases for MPEG4 when MT-based cache locking is used. However, the decrease is more for MT-based I1 cache locking (MT is at level-1 cache). For I1/CL2 from 2/64 KB to 32/1024 KB, mean delay per task is decreased by 38% and total power consumption is decreased by 32% for MPEG4 (see Table **2**, Figs. **5** and **6**). For FFT, MT-based I1/CL2 cache locking has no positive impact on mean delay per task, but total power consumption increases about 12% for I1/CL2 size increases from 2/64 KB to 32/1024 KB regardless cache locking is done at I1 or at CL2.

Table 2: Changes due to 25% I1/CL2 Cache Locking with MT at either CL1 or CL2 Levels

Parameters (Range of value)	App. Name	Changes (%)			
		Delay		Power	
		MT/Lock at I1	MT/Lock at CL2	MT/Lock at I1	MT/Lock at CL2
I1/CL2 size (KB) (2/64 – 32/1024)	MPEG4	(-)38%	(-)33%	(-)32%	(-)30%
	FFT	0	0	(+)12%	(+)12%
Line size (Byte) (16 – 256)	MPEG4	(-)28%	(-)26%	(-)27%	(-)25%
	FFT	0	0	0	0
Assoc. level (1-way – 16-way)	MPEG4	(-)33%	(-)31%	(-)30%	(-)28%
	FFT	0	0	0	0

CONCLUSION

Traditional single-core processors are not capable of supporting future complex computing. Multicore architectures provide a new platform in implementing highly completed algorithms. Multicore architectures have multilevel caches and caches are power hungry and make the execution time unpredictability even worse. Various cache locking techniques are used in single-core system to improve predictability and performance and to decrease total power consumption. However, implementing cache locking in multicore architecture is very challenging because of the architectural complexity.

Previously we introduced an efficient block selection methodology based on the number of cache misses by each block. We also introduced Miss Table (MT)-based cache locking scheme where information about the blocks and the cache misses are stored in a Miss Table to facilitate the cache locking. Miss Table information can also be used to improve victim block selection performance. Cache locking in multicore is more challenging because of the complexity introduced by multicore architecture. Therefore, it is important and difficult to know whether Miss Tables at level-1 caches or Miss Table at level-2 cache has a better impact on predictability and performance/power ratio. In this Chapter, we investigate the impact of Miss Table-based cache locking at level-1 and Miss Table-based cache locking at level-2 on the predictability and performance/power ratio.

We use VisualSim to model an 8-core architecture, where each core's private cache (*i.e.*, level-1 cache) is split into instruction cache (I1) and data cache (D1) and level-2 cache (CL2) is unified and shared by the cores. We use Heptane to generate workload for MPEG4 decoding and FFT algorithms to run the simulation program. Experimental results show that a maximum reduction of 38% in mean delay per task and a maximum reduction of 32% in total power consumption are achieved by locking one-fourth of the I1 cache size for MPEG4. Whereas, a maximum reduction of 33% in mean delay per task and a maximum reduction of 30% in total power consumption are achieved by locking one-fourth of the CL2 cache size for MPEG4. Therefore, Miss Table based cache locking at level-1 is more beneficiary than Miss Table based cache locking at level-2 for MPEG4. Simulation results also show that Miss Table-based cache locking at level-1 and Miss Table based cache locking at level-2 have almost the same impact on the mean delay per task and total power consumption for FFT (and similar workloads whose code entirely fits in the I1). Even though total power consumption decreases at the beginning (2/64 KB to 4/128 KB) for FFT, it starts increasing with the increase of I1/CL2 size from 4/128 KB. This is because small sized FFT code does not take advantage of higher cache sizes (and MT-based cache locking at I1/CL2). This leads to the idea of saving power by disabling the miss table for small workloads such as FFT.

We plan to investigate the impact of adding a Miss Table on the victim cache (between CL1 and CL2) performance as an extension of this work in the near future.

APPENDIX

Appendix A: VisualSim Block Diagram

Fig. **A** shows the model of simulated multicore architecture with 8 cores using VisualSim blocks. In VisualSim, a computing system is described in three major parts – Architecture, Behavior, and Workload. Architecture includes elements like processing core, cache, bus, and main memory. Behavior describes the actions performed on the system. Examples include network traffic shaping. Workload is the transactions that traverse the system such as network traffic.

Appendix B: VisualSim Simulation Cockpit

Fig. **B** shows the VisualSim Simulation Cockpit. The Simulation Cockpit provides functionalities (left-top in the Figure) to run the model and to collect simulation results (right side in the Figure). Parameters can be changed before running the simulation without modifying the block diagram. The final results can be saved into text/graph files and/or printed for further analysis.

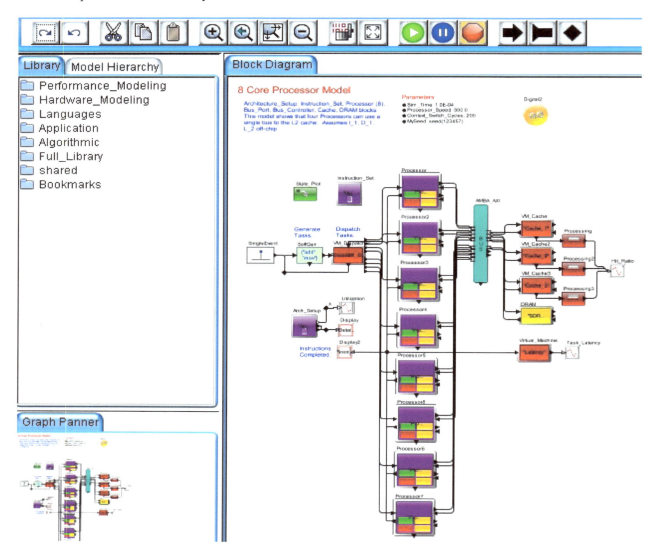

Figure A: VisualSim Model.

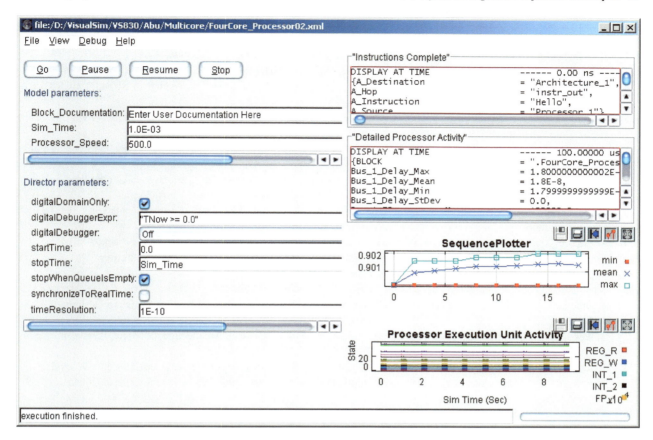

Figure B: VisualSim Simulation Cockpit.

REFERENCES

[1]   Suhendra V, Mitra T. Exploring Locking & Partitioning for Predictable Shared Caches on Multi-Cores. In the Proceedings of DAC'08; Anaheim, CA, 2008.

[2]   Asaduzzaman A, Mahgoub I. Cache Modeling and Optimization for Portable Devices Running MPEG-4 Video Decoder. J Multimed Tools Applica; 2006, 239-256.

[3]   Asaduzzaman A, Sibai F.N. Improving Cache Locking Performance of Modern Embedded Systems *via* the Addition of a Miss Table at the L2 Cache Level, Journal of System Architectures (JSA), Accepted, Feb. 2010.

[4]   Puaut I. Cache Analysis Vs Static Cache Locking for Schedulability Analysis in Multitasking Real-Time Systems. 2006. http://www.cs.york.ac.uk/rts/wcet2002/papers/puaut.pdf

[5]   Puaut I, Decotigny D. Low-Complexity Algorithms for Static Cache Locking in Multitasking Hard RT Systems. In IEEE Real-Time Systems Symposium; 2002, 241–268.

[6]   Puaut I, Pais C. Scratchpad memories vs locked caches in hard real-time systems: a quantitative comparison. In Design, Automation & Test in Europe Conference & Exhibition; 2007, 1-6.

[7]   Tarui T, Nakagawa T, Ido N, *et al.* Evaluation of the lock mechanism in a snooping cache. In ACM Proceedings of the 6th international conference on Supercomputing. 1992.

[8]   Tamura E, Rodriguez F, Busquets-Mataix JV, *et al.* High Performance Memory Architectures with Dynamic Locking Cache for Real-Time Systems, In the Proceedings of the 16th Euromicro Conference on Real-Time Systems; Italy, 2004, 1-4.

[9]   Harrison C. Programming the cache on the PowerPC 750GX/FX - Use cache management instructions to improve performance. In IBM Microcontroller Applications Group; 2005. http://www-128.ibm.com/ developerworks/library/pa-ppccache.html

[10]   Stokes J. Xenon's L2 vs. Cell's local storage, and some notes on IBM/Nintendo's Gekko; 2005. http://arstechnica.com/articles/paedia/cpu/xbox360-1.ars/6

[11]   Smart Cache. 2008. Cache - Smart Computing Encyclopedia http://www.smartcomputing.com/editorial/dictionary/detail. asp?guid= &searchtype=&DicID=16600&RefType=Encyclopedia

[12]   Romanchenko V. Quad-Core Opteron: architecture and roadmaps. Digital-Daily.com; 2006.

[13]   Torres G. Inside Pentium 4 Architecture. Hardware Secrets, LLC; 2005. http://www.hardwaresecrets.com/printpage/235/1

[14]   Vera X., Lisper, B. Data Cache Locking for Higher Program Predictability. In the Proceedings of SIGMETRICS'03; CA, 2003.

[15]   Arnaud A, Puaut I. Dynamic Instruction Cache Locking in Hard Real-Time Systems; 2005. http://www.irisa.fr/caps/ publications/pdfs/arnaud-Locking.pdf

[16]   Tamura E, Busquets-Mataix JV, Martin, JJS, *et al.* A Comparison of Three Genetic Algorithms for Locking-Cache Contents Selection in Real-Time Systems. In the Proceedings of the International Conference in Coimbra; Portugal, 2005.

[17]   Campoy AM, Tamura E, Saez S, *et al.* On Using Locking Caches in Embedded Real-Time Systems. In the Proceedings of ICESS-05, LNCS 3820, 2005. 150-159.

[18]   Romanchenko V. Evaluation of the multi-core processor architecture Intel core: Conroe, Kentsfield... In Digital-Daily.com; 2006.

[19]   Multicore. 2008. Multi-core (computing) http://en. wikipedia.org/wiki/Xeon; http://en.wikipedia.org/ wiki/Athlon

[20]   Every DK. IBM's Cell Processor: The next generation of computing? In Shareware Press; 2005. http://www.mymac.com/fileupload/CellProcessor.pdf

[21]   Sibai FN. On the Performance Benefits of Sharing and Privatizing Second and Third Level Cache Memories in Homogeneous Multi-Core Architectures. In Microprocessors and Microsystems, Embedded Hardware Design, 2008, 32, 405-412.

[22]   Stokes J. Introducing the IBM/Sony/Toshiba Cell Processor – Part II: The Cell Architecture; 2005. http://arstechnica.com/ articles/ paedia/cpu/cell-2.ars

[23]   Blachford N. Cell Architecture Explained Version 2; 2006. http://www.blachford.info/computer/Cell/Cell0_v2.html

[24]   Vance A. Cell processor goes commando. Mountain View; 2006. http://www.theregister.co.uk/2006/01/22/cell_ mecury_army/

[25]   VisualSim. 2010. A system-level simulator from Mirabilis Design, Inc. http://www.mirabilisdesign.com/

[26]   Heptane. 2010. A tree-based WCET analysis tool. http://ralyx.inria.fr/2004/Raweb/aces/uid43.html

[27]   Asaduzzaman A, Mahgoub I, Sibai FN. Impact of L1 Entire Locking and L2 Way Locking on Performance, Power Consumption, and Predictability of Multicore Real-Time Systems. In the Proceedings of IEEE AICCSA'09; 2009, Rabat, Morocco.

CHAPTER 3

TRoCMP: An Approach to Energy Saving for Multi-Core Systems

Long Zheng[1,2], Mianxiong Dong[1,3], Minyi Guo[*,4], Song Guo[1], Kaoru Ota[1,3], and Jun Ma[1]

[1]*School of Computer Science and Engineering, University of Aizu, Aizu-Wakamatsu, 965-8580, Japan;* [2]*School of Computer Science and Technology, Huazhong University of Science and Technology, 430074, China;* [3]*Department of Electrical and Computer Engineering, University of Waterloo, Waterloo, N2L, 3G1, Canada and* [4]*Department of Computer Science and Engineering, Shanghai Jiao Tong University, Shanghai, 200020, China*

Abstract: Nowadays, multi-core processor, also called Chip Multiprocessor (CMP) becomes the mainstream that can achieve higher computation capability. However, energy issue is still a crucial problem for design and manufacture of multi-core processor. Tag reduction technique can save energy of the single-core system. This chapter introduces the Tag Reduction on CMP (TRoCMP) that is a novel approach to energy saving for multi-core system. We first extend tag reduction from single-core to multi-core processor, including proposing 3 heuristic algorithms to implement TRoCMP. Then the performance overhead is considered, so that Core Degree mechanism and a refined heuristic algorithm are further introduced and designed to find out the trade-off of energy saving and performance overhead of TRoCMP. In particular, we formulate the energy consumption and performance overhead of TRoCMP to analyze and estimate them. In experiments, we modify the Linux kernel and implement new modules to collect the experimental data from benchmarks of SPEC CPU2006 running on a real operating system. In this way, the precision of our experiments is guaranteed, since tag reduction is very sensitive to the usage of physical memory. The experimental results show that our TRoCMP can save total energy up to 83.93% and 76.16% on 8-core and 4-core processors in average respectively, compared to the one that the tag-reduction is not used for. TRoCMP outperforms significantly tag reduction on single-core processor as well. With consideration of performance overhead, when Core Degree is set to 6, the best balance of energy saving and performance overhead can be achieved.

INTRODUCTION

Over the last decade, manufacturers competed to advance the performance of processors by raising the clock frequency. However, the dramatically increased power consumption and thermal problem caused by high clock frequency have ended this race. Now duplicating a number of cores in a chip, called Chip Multiprocessor (CMP) [1], as multi-core processor, is considered as an easier and more efficient way to enhance the perfor-mance of microprocessors. Multi-core architecture is quickly becoming the mainstream that can achieve higher computational capacity. Intel has acclaimed that more than 64 cores will be integrated into one processor in the near future [2]. Nvidia has presented its may-core solution-GPGPU [3]. Moreover the multi-core architecture that is applied to embedded system and mobile computing has emerged recently [4].

It is widely known that the cache system is one of most power consuming component in any computer processor, as it is implemented as SRAM in order to get a fast clock frequency. Taking two widely-used commercial processors as example, the cache system in Alpha 21164 uses up to 25% of the total energy consumed by the processor [5], and even higher in StrongARM-110 with the Instruction Cache (I-Cache) and Data Cache (D-Cache) of up to 26% and 17% [6], respectively. The less power dissipation means to relieve the thermal problem and prolong the battery lifetime in hand-held devices. Whereas, saving energy usually leads to performance degradation, so the energy and performance are always two major issues that should be well balanced in design and optimization of micro-processors.

Tag reduction technique is one of efficient methods to save energy consumed by processors, especially by the one of cache system. Recent research based on tag reduction is only for single-core processors. This motivates us to further explore the tag reduction technique for Level 1 Instruction Cache (L1 I-Cache) of a multi-core processor. In this chapter, our Tag Reduction on CMP (TRoCMP) is introduced to apply tag reduction to multi-core processors. Both energy saving and performance overhead of TRoCMP are discussed.

*****Address correspondence to Dr. Minyi Guo:** Department of Computer Science and Engineering, Shanghai Jiao Tong University, Shanghai, 200240, China; Email: guo-my@cs.sjtu.edu.cn

First we exploit the energy saving of TRoCMP. Because of features of the multi-core processor, it can save more energy to use tag reduction technique on multi-core processor than the one on last generation processor, *i.e.* single-core pro-cessor. With the multi-core processor, we can assign the physical pages residing in physical memory to different core to improve the effect of energy saving by tag reduction, followed by formulating the energy consumption of TRoCMP to an equivalent problem which is to find an assignment of the whole instruction pages in the physical memory to a set of cores such that the tag-reduction conflicts for each core can be mostly avoided or reduced. We then propose a group of algorithms using three heuristics for this assignment problem to implement our TRoCMP.

Nevertheless, TRoCMP causes the extra context switches as the overhead to assign instruction pages to multiple cores. After the analysis of performance overhead of TRoCMP, the Core Degree that is defined as the number of cores that tag reduction can use for each application is introduced. With the Core Degree mechanism, both energy consumption and performance overhead of TRoCMP are decided as functions of the Core Degree. The Core Degree constraint controls the overhead at all acceptable level by restricting of the number of cores that the instruction page frames are allowed to. Then, a refined heuristic algorithm is proposed and added to TRoCMP to implement the Core Degree mechanism. By varying the values of Core Degree, we can find out the most appropriate value of Core Degree that can achieve the best balance of energy saving and performance cost from our experimental results.

Besides, it is difficult to get comprehensive data to measure the trade-off of energy saving and performance overhead directly. Instead, we develop a model that can evaluate both energy saving and performance overhead of tag reduction quantitatively. As a result the design and implementation of our experiment can be much simplified.

In the experiments, we do not adopt the method widely used in previous micro-processor architecture research in which some processor simulator is used as experimental platform to collect data. There are two reasons. One is that the results of tag reduction relies on the real distribution of instruction page frames, so it is crucial to collect the distribution information of instruction page frames residing in physical memory. The other one is that previous research on tag reduction only considers one thread behavior, which is far different from real operating system environment on multi-core processor. The traditional processor simulator cannot fully support both the processes switch and detailed memory hierarchy. In our experiments, we modify the Linux kernel and implement new modules to collect the experimental data from benchmarks of SPEC CPU2006 [7] running on a real operating system, which assures and validates the precision of our experimental results.

The remainder of this chapter is structured as follows. Section 2 briefly presents the related research on tag reduction and other work on energy saving. Section 3 introduces the knowledge of virtual address, cache and tag that are fundamental of energy saving of tag reduction. Section 4 proposes the methodology of TRoCMP. Section 5 and 6 describe and analyze TRoCMP in details from view of energy saving and performance overhead respectively. Furthermore, the experimental results also are in Section 5 and 6 to evaluate the TRoCMP. Section 7 summarizes our findings and concludes the chapter.

RELATED WORK

In this section, we first review the previous research on tag reduction, and other related techniques on energy savings are also discussed.

Tag reduction is a way to save energy consumed by L1 Cache and the Table Lookaside Buffer (TLB) in a processor [8-11]. It has received much attention in the literature because it can save energy of caches significantly. Tag reduction has been applied to general or customizable embedded processor [8, 10], to the TLB [9], as well as to the processor using heterogeneously tagged caches [11]. Most research effects of tag reduction focus on its utilization on a single-core processor.

Other approaches to energy reduction of cache system have been also investigated. Inoue *et al* [12] and McNairy *et al* [13] proposed the dynamic reduction to reduce the energy consumption of set-associative cache access in L1 and L2 caches, respectively. Way prediction first appeared in the R10000 processor [12, 14]. Kessler *et al* [15] and Tang *et al* [16] implemented the way prediction in L1 I-Cache and in the branch buffer. A multiple-MRU predictor proposed in [17] offers higher prediction accuracy. The gated-Vdd [18] gates the power supply to the cache lines that are not likely to be accessed. The gated-Vss [19] disconnects the ground connection to turn off the lines. A similar method in [20] powers off the cache lines containing the data which are not useful. Instead of turning off cache lines completely, Drowsy cache [21] just adjusts the supply voltage of cache lines. The Multiple MRU policy [22] is proposed to reduce the wake-up delay of Drowsy cache. Tam *et al* [23] exploits reuse information to reduce the overheads caused by the state change of cache lines.

Besides the techniques for cache system as just surveyed, many other energy saving methods and algorithms have been also proposed. For example, Dynamic Voltage Scaling (DVS) [24-26] is a common methodology to save processor energy. With support of multi-level voltage of a modern processor, it can decrease the power dissipation of a processor by adapting voltage level of a processor for different parts of a program. The lower voltage, the less energy is consumed. The methods proposed in [25, 26] extend DVS [24] to CMP by exploring extra potentials for the energy saving with the characteristics of CMP. Another group work concentrates on energy saving for memory hierarchy. The modern physical memory DRAM technology has well developed to provide up to six low power modes [27], which allows advanced methods and algorithms e.g. [28-30] to adjust to DRAM power mode during the execution of programs in real time.

VIRTUAL ADDRESS, CACHE AND TAG

Before describing the TRoCMP, it is necessary to slow down our presentation to explain tag reduction. The fundamental of energy saving by tag reduction is based on the memory hierarchy of operation system and the organization of caches of a processor. Therefore, virtual address, cache and tag are firstly introduced conceptually.

Virtual Address

Modern processor and operating system usually use three kinds of address to finally access the physical memory: logical address, virtual address and physical address.

The logical address is a static address depending on compilers, which is not supported by all computer architectures. Intel's x86 family processor uses logical address, but others, taking MIPS architecture processors for example. The corresponding operating systems have to fit the different choice of using logical address. Windows family operating sys-tems fully support the logical address, however most UNIX and UNIX-like operating systems do not support it or support it partially. With help of segment mechanism, the logical address needs to be translated into the virtual address that is used by a processor.

The virtual address is used by a processor in order to achieve the best utilization of physical memory. With a general 32-bit processor without Physical Address Extension (PAE), each process has a separate 32-bit virtual address space, so each process seems to have 4GB memory although the actual physical memory does not have so large capacity and all the processes actually share the precious physical memory. With help of page mechanism, virtual address can extend the capacity of physical memory; with help of page swapping mechanism, virtual address can support swapping out some useless data to hard disk, so as to save more valuable physical memory. Almost all processors use virtual address except some embedded processors that are limited by their simple architecture.

Physical memory is where the data and instructions reside actually. When a processor accesses the memory, a mechanism of translating the virtual address into physical address is needed. Page table and Translation Lookaside Buffer (TLB) implement this function. Each process has a page table to record the pairs of a virtual address and the corresponding physical address. Page table system is maintained by operating system, and used by an operating system and a processor. However the page table is stored in physical memory, a processor need to read it very frequently, and reading data from physical memory needs much time. Therefore, most modern processors have a cache-like component called TLB to cache some latest used page table entries to speed up the translation from virtual address into physical address.

Cache and Tag

As mentioned above, accessing physical memory need much time, it is very efficient to cache some latest used instruction and data. In a modern processor, the cache system becomes more and more complicated, and it influences the per-formance of the processor directly and significantly. In most general processor, there are two or even three levels of cache to speed up the access to physical memory. Level 2 (L2) and Level 3 (L3) cache, if it exists, use physical address to access data, but Level 1 (L1) cache has option whether it uses physical address or virtual address.

As there are several options to access the L1 caches by different addresses. The processor can use the virtual address to access caches directly, but it brings the synonym problem which may result in wasting some precious L1 cache resources. Alternatively, it is also possible to access the caches by physical address because the instructions and data are actually stored there. The synonym problem can be avoided, however, the processor needs to translate the virtual address to physical address in advance, which delays the accessing to L1 caches and degrades the performance of L1 caches. As a result, most of modern general processors adopt a mixed way that virtual address is used to index an entry of L1 caches while the physical address is translated by the TLB concurrently. Such physical address will be used to compare against the tag in the indexed entry in order to solve the synonym problem. This kind of L1 cache is called Virtually-Indexed Physically-Tagged (VIPT) cache. Similarly, the other two mentioned earlier are called Virtually-Indexed Virtually-Tagged (VIVT) cache and Physically-Indexed Physically-Tagged (PIPT) cache, respectively.

This chapter focuses on the optimization of VIPT L1 Instruction Cache (I-Cache) and similar approach can apply to L1 Data Cache (D-Cache) as well. The concept of virtual address, L1 I-Cache, Instruction TLB (I-TLB) and the tag mechanism are illustrated in Fig. **1**. Without lose of generality, the organization of the VIPT L1 I-Cache is based on a 32-bit processor model and some less related technical details like L2 TLBs are omitted.

When the processor accesses the L1 I-Cache, the 32-bit virtual address is divided into two parts. The most significant 20 bits constitute the Virtual Page Number (VPN) and the remainder is the page offset which is further divided into two 6-bit parts. The lower 6 bits are sent to processor directly, while the higher 6 bits are used as index to access the corresponding entry of the L1 I-Cache. Mean-while, VPN is translated into physical page number (PPN) through the TLB. Each entry of L1 I-Cache is composed by a tag and instructions. The tag stores the PPN of these instructions. Only if the tag in the entry is equal to the PPN translated by the TLB, called as L1 I-Cache hit, the instructions in the entry indexed by the most significant 6 bits of page offset are confirmed to be what the processor really needs to access. Otherwise, the L1 I-Cache miss leads to the secondary access to L2 I-Cache.

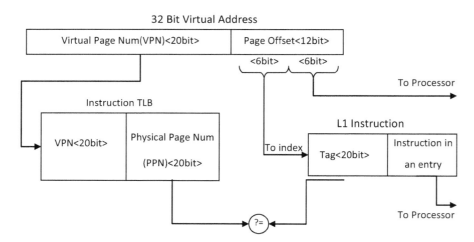

Figure 1: The organization of VIPT L1 cache.

METHODOLOGY OF TROCMP

The previous research on tag reduction shows a significant effect of energy saving of L1 caches of a single-core processor. Whereas, drawbacks due to features and constraints of the single-core processor do exist. TRoCMP applies tag reduction to multi-core processors, so that we can investigate the more opportunities of the tag reduction for energy saving. In this section, we first introduce the fundamental of energy saving of tag reduction. After analyzing the drawbacks of tag reduction on single-core processor, the overview of TRoCMP is presented.

Tag Reduction

A modern 32-bit processor with or without PAE can support up to 64GB or 4GB physical memory, respectively. Because operating system does not always exhaust all the physical memory, especially when PAE enable, it is a kind of waste to use 20-bit tag to distinguish the entries that have the same page offset.

The tag is implemented as SRAM in order to achieve a fast clock. The organization of the tag hardware in a cache is illustrated in Fig. **2** [10]. The tag is an array which includes several entries. All bits in a tag entry reside in a wordline. Each time when the tag entry is accessed, all bitlines are charged first and then discharged. If the bit stays at a high voltage level, it represents 1; otherwise 0. After a cycle of charging and discharging, the wordline of this tag entry returns the bits. That is why tag consumes so much energy.

According to the organization of tag hardware, if the length a tag needs can be reduced, the unnecessary bitlines can be prevented from being accessed, so that the total energy consumption of tag can be decreased. This is the fundamental of energy saving by tag reduction.

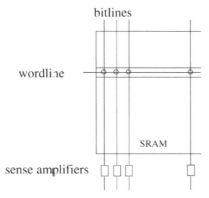

Figure 2: The hardware of the tag organization.

The effect of tag reduction highly relies on the number and location distribution of page frames in physical memory. In the best-case scenario, the number of bits a tag needs to distinguish all page frames in physical memory, B_{single}^{best}, can be calculated as

$$B_{single}^{best} = \log_2 N \tag{1}$$

where N is the total number of page frames in physical memory. So theoretically, the larger the number of page frames is, the more bits of the tag are needed. Whereas, it is not always true in the real situation, as the entire page frames are not consecutive in the physical memory.

Drawbacks of Tag Reduction on Single-core Processors

An example of physical memory with 16 page frames illustrated in Fig. **3** offers us an inside observation of what happens when the tag reduction is used to analyze the drawbacks of tag reduction on a single-core processor. In both graphs of Fig. **3**, each cell represents a page frame in physical memory. The gray cells, called the Instruction Page (I-Page) frames, represent page frames containing instructions; the white ones represent free page frames or non-instruction page frames. The number on the left side of each page frame is its physical page number. The number on the right side of each I-Page frame is the physical page number after tag reduction. It is easy to find out from Fig. **3(a)** that instead of using 20-bit tag in L1 I-Cache, only 3 bits are enough to distinguish all the 6 I-Page frames. So the bits of tag can be reduced without incurring any side effect. This is equal to the best scenario described above. The same conclusion may not be achieved from different distribution of I-Page frames. As we observed in Fig. **3(b)**, in which there are still 6 page frames used, if only 3 bits are used, the reduced tag can not distinguish all these 6 page frames, e.g. page frames 0101 and 1101 This is called tag-reduction conflict. To solve this problem in this example, at least 4 bits are needed to distinguish all I-Page frames.

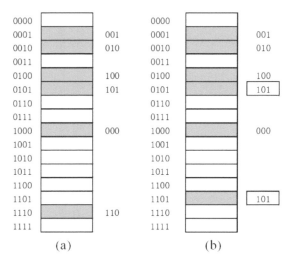

(a)   (b)

Figure 3: Examples of tag reduction technique applying to physical memory. (a) is the diagram of physical memory which needs 3 bits to distinguish all pages used. (b) is the diagram of physical memory which needs 4 bits to distinguish all pages used due to the tag-reduction conflict.

From the above examples, we can find out when the I-Page frames are not consecutive, the shortest tag-length depends on the distribution of the I-Page frames in the physical memory. In the best case, there is no difference from the case that all I-Page frames are consecutive. On the contrary, in the worst scenario, the length of the tag that is required to distinguish all page frames in physical memory, B_{single}^{worst}, is

$$B_{single}^{worst} = \log_2(|\xi_{bottom} - \xi_{top}|) \tag{2}$$

where ξ_{top} is the physical address of the page frame that resides in the top of physical memory, ξ_{bottom} is the physical address of the page frame that resides in the bottom of physical memory.

However in real operating system, taking Linux for example, the distribution of physical memory is more complicated than above, since the operating system is lazy. When a process begins to execute, the operating system only creates a virtual address space for this process rather than loads instructions and data into physical memory. When this process needs to access the physical memory for some data or instructions that are not loaded, a page fault occurs. Then operating system will load the page the process needs and several nearby pages, which is called pre-loading. On the other hand, if the instructions or data in a page are not used for a long time, and the capacity of free sys-tem physical memory is low, this page will be swapped out of the physical memory address or even swapped to hard disk. And when a process terminates, all pages of this process will be swapped out. With the policy of the use of physical memory, the I-Page frames can be consecutive locally because of pre-loading but discrete globally because of page swapping mechanism, multi-process running on the same system simultaneously, and the natural difference between I-Page frame and Date Page (D-Page) frame.

Therefore, on the single-core processor, the tag in L1 I-Cache has to distinguish the whole of I-Page frames residing in physical memory, as well as the L1 D-Cache does. Furthermore, based on the analysis of the function of the operation system, the distribution of page frames in physical memory is dynamic and is hardly controllable by users in the computer system using virtual address mechanism and VIPT L1 Cache, the approach of the previous work on the tag reduction of a single-core processor is to use more bits of tag to distinguish all page frames in physical memory when the tag-reduction conflict occurs. In some extreme scenario, the tag may not be possible to be reduced at all because of the tag-reduction conflict.

Overview of TRoCMP

The drawbacks of tag reduction on the single-core processor inspire us to apply the tag reduction to the multi-core processor and to investigate the potential of energy saving of the multi-core processor with tag reduction.

The multi-core architecture brings the Thread Level Parallelism (TLP) instead of the Instruction Level Parallelism (ILP) which is one of major ways to improve performance of a single-core processor. While a thread is always called a light-weighted process, there are two major differences between a thread and a process. One is that a process can consist of several threads or have only one thread itself. The other is that threads belonging to the same process share their memory address space. In other words, all these threads can access or modify the data in the shared memory address space. On the contrary, each process has its own separated memory address space and if other wants to access its memory address space, most of time, it causes a fatal error. Nevertheless, except for the differences above, operating system does not distinguish them. Especially in process scheduling, operating system treats threads and processes the same way. Since these differences do not affect the discussion of this chapter, from now we do not distinguish a thread and a process explicitly, and we use the same word *thread* to represent them, except for some special cases when we need to distinguish them.

There are multiple cores in a multi-core processor; therefore two or more threads can run parallel on different cores. This is how multi-core processor gains performance improvement. Nevertheless, TLP on multi-core processor would be much complicated. In order to decrease cache missing and achieve further optimization of each core, multi-core processor with the support of operating system enables an affiliation mechanism that dedicates each thread running on a particular core, just like that each thread affiliates to a particular core. Since Windows NT 4.0 and Linux 2.4 supported Shared Memory Multiprocessor (SMP), implying that they also support multi-core processor, the affiliation mechanism has been implemented. Because of affiliation mechanism, in the real multi-core system, all I-Pages of a thread are assigned to a particular core, and the thread always runs on this core.

The conventional optimization for the multi-core processor is to improve the threads parallelism by generating more threads running simultaneously on multiple cores. From a different optimization consideration, we assign different parts of all instructions residing in physical memory to the cores in the way that can achieve the best benefits by exploring the tag-reduction technique.

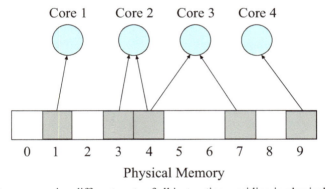

Figure 4: The idea of different cores running different parts of all instructions residing in physical memory.

Fig. **4** conceptually depicts how to assign pages containing instructions to different cores. Numbers from 0 to 9 are the physical page numbers. The arrows from an I-Page frame to a core denote the assignment, which means the specific core executes the instructions in a specific page frame. For example, Page 1 is assigned to Core 1 only and Page 4 is assigned to both Cores 2 and 3. The pages assigned to different cores may not be executed simultaneously because the execution needs keep the same sequence of a thread as the one without tag reduction. However, it is no harmful for the parallelism of a multi-core processor, since there are numerous threads running on the operation system in which cores execute the instructions of pages belonging to the different threads, at any time.

Different from the traditional shared memory processor, the multi-core processor is more flexible to organize its cache hierarchy by exploiting the shared caches since all cores are integrated to a single chip. For example, some kinds of multi-core processors share L2 caches, while others may only allow sharing L3 cache. No matter how they share their L2 or L3 caches, the L1 caches are always private for each core. Since L1 I-Cache of each core is private and each core processes a subset of all instructions in physical memory, the tag in each core only needs to distinguish the corresponding subset of all physical memory page numbers, resulting in that the length of tag can be further reduced.

In the conventional research on tag reduction of single-core processor, the tag-reduction conflicts can only be decided by distribution of page frames that controlled by operating system and the status of current physical memory. There is no potential to decrease the probability of tag-reduction conflict. In multi-core architecture, as each core has its private L1 I-Cache, and different I-Page frames can be assigned to different cores, the occurrences of tag-reduction conflicts can be greatly decreased or even avoided. With the two reasons above, in a word, tag reduction technique can save more energy for the multi-core processor.

We first consider the ideal case that no tag-reduction conflicts will occur, when the tag reduction is applied to multi-core processor. Under such considerations, tag size B^i_{cmp} of each core i is

$$\begin{cases} B^i_{cmp} = \log_2 N_i \\ N = \sum_{i=0}^{w} N_i \end{cases} \tag{3}$$

where N_i is the number of page frames assigned to core i, N is the number of all page frames in physical memory and w is the number of the cores. With mathematics, when each N_i is equal to each other, each B^i_{cmp} can get minimal. Obviously, B^i_{cmp} is always smaller than B^{best}_{single}, and then tag reduction on multi-core processor benefits from the smaller number of page frames assigned to each core, resulting in an improved energy saving.

ENERGY SAVING OF TROCMP

Energy Analysis

Recall that accessing a tag once undergoes a cycle of charging and discharging as described in Section 4.1. We assume the energy consumption of one such cycle for one bit tag to be e Joules. When programs run on a processor, some instructions are jumped over and, on the contrary, some are executed repeatedly. However, the instructions are executed by a processor like an instruction flow from view of the processor. Each instruction fetching from cache and memory hierarchy needs to access L1 I-Cache tag. Because the execution of different instructions takes different time, the number of instructions executed in a processor time slice may be not equal.

For a multi-core processor with w cores, running t threads, the energy consumption E on the L1 I-Cache tag in a period with s time slices can be calculated as follows.

$$E = e \cdot \sum_{i=1}^{s} \sum_{j=1}^{w} \sum_{n=1}^{a_{ij}} TagR(\bigcup_{m=1}^{t} AddEx(I_{ij}(m,n))) \tag{4}$$

The variables and functions in (4) are detailed as follows. $\forall i, 1 \leq i \leq s$ and $\forall m, 1 \leq m \leq t$, we use $I_{ij}(m,n)$ to denote a set that represents thread m's instruction flow till the n-th instruction executed by the j-th core during the i-th time slice. Each element records a particular instruction's physical address and executed time. In the instruction flow, the element of $I_{ij}(m,n)$ is a two-dimensional array, just like (A,T) in which A is the physical address and T is the executed time. The n-th instruction can be expressed as (A_n, T_n). Therefore thread m's instruction flow till the n-th instruction can be expressed exactly as

$$\{(A,T)|(A,T) \in I'_{ij}(m), T \leq T_n\} \tag{5}$$

where $I'_{ij}(m)$ represents thread m's instruction flow executed by the j-th core during the i-th time slice.

Function $AddEx$ is to extract the A of each (A,T) of set $I_{ij}(m)$ to compose a new physical address set. Function $TagR$ is to reduce the length of tag with the physical address set $AddEx(I_{ij}(m))$. Furthermore, a_{ij} is the total number of instructions executed by the j-th core, during the i-th time slice, *i.e.*

$$a_{ij} = num(\bigcup_{m=1}^{t} I'_{ij}(m)) \tag{6}$$

We further define the average number of bits that a tag requires after tag reduction for the *j-th* core to execute all the instructions in the *i-th* time slide, $\overline{B_{ij}}$, as follows.

$$\overline{B_{ij}} = \frac{1}{a_{ij}} \cdot \sum_{n=1}^{a_{ij}} TagR(\bigcup_{m=1}^{t} AddEx(I_{ij}(m,n))) \tag{7}$$

Equation (4) can thus be rewritten as

$$E = e \cdot \sum_{i=1}^{s} \sum_{j=1}^{w} (\overline{B_{ij}} \cdot a_{ij}) \tag{8}$$

Let N_i be the total number of instructions executed by all cores in the *i-th* time slice, *i.e.*,

$$N_i = \sum_{j=1}^{w} a_{ij} \tag{9}$$

and f_{ij} be the ratio of the number of instructions assigned to the *j-th* core over the total number of instructions to all cores in the *i-th* time slice, *i.e.*,

$$f_{ij} = \frac{a_{ij}}{\sum_{j=1}^{w} a_{ij}} = \frac{a_{ij}}{N_i} \tag{10}$$

Equation (4) can be eventually expressed as

$$E = e \cdot \sum_{i=1}^{s} \sum_{j=1}^{w} (\overline{B_{ij}} \cdot f_{ij} \cdot N_i) \tag{11}$$

If we define

$$N_{max} \equiv \max_{1 \le i \le s} (N_i) \tag{12}$$

the upper bound of energy consumption by tag reduction $\mathcal{E}$ can be derived as

$$E \le \mathcal{E} = e \cdot N_{max} \cdot \sum_{i=1}^{s} \sum_{j=1}^{w} (\overline{B_{ij}} \cdot f_{ij}) \tag{13}$$

We've obtained the upper bound of energy consumption with tag reduction under the Core Degree constraints as formulated in (13). The upper bound of energy consumption can be calculated if $\overline{B_{ij}}$ and f_{ij} are known, since both e and N_{max} are constant numbers.

Heuristic Algorithms

Applying tag reduction to a multi-core processor has two more potentials to enhance the effect of tag reduction compared to the one to single-core processor. One is that as each core has its own private L1 I-Cache, the number of I-Page frames assigned to each core decreases, so that the necessary number of bits of tag is less. The other one is that operating system can decide which core an I-Page frame should be assigned to, to avoid tag-reduction conflicts.

Based on the analysis above, we propose 3 algorithms to implement TRoCMP. All of 3 algorithms enable the core affiliation, which is a trend that when a new page of instructions loaded into physical memory, it will be assigned to the core to which the last I-Page frame was assigned to. In our 3 algorithms, the core affiliation only effects when the core affiliation cannot influence the original algorithm result which should be when the core affiliation is disabled. 3 algorithms will be demonstrated as follows.

Random Assignment with No Priority (RANP) Algorithm

This algorithm is the simplest algorithm. When operating system loads a new page of instructions to physical memory, it just assigns this I-Page frame to a random core. The details of RANP algorithm can be described into the following steps.

(1) Load a page of instructions into an I-Page frame whose page frame number is N.

(2) Find out which core I-Page frame N-1 was assigned to. If the core is found, then go to Step 3, otherwise go to Step 4.

(3) Assign I-Page frame N to the core just found. Then go to step 5.

(4) Assign I-Page frame N to the random core.

(5) Reduce tag.

(6) If more pages of instruction are needed to load into physical memory, return to Step 1; otherwise end.

RANP algorithm only decreases the number of I-Page frames which are assigned to each core, but does not consider the tag-reduction conflicts.

Conflict-Aware Assignment with Workload Priority (CAWP) Algorithm

In CAWP algorithm, which core an I-Page frame should be assigned to depends on the number of I-Page frames of each core. Following steps show the detail of CAWP algorithm.

(1) Load a page of instructions into an I-Page frame whose page frame number is N.

(2) Find out which cores have the smallest number of I-Page frames assigned. If only one core is found, assign I-Page frame N to the core found; otherwise, go to Step 3.

(3) Check whether the core where I-Page frame N-1 was assigned is in the result of Step 2. If it is, assign I-Page frame N to the core where I-Page frame N-1 was assigned; otherwise assign I-Page frame N to random cores in the result.

(4) Reduce tag.

(5) If more pages of instruction are needed to load into physical memory, return to Step 1; otherwise end.

CAWP algorithm focuses on the number of I-Page frames assigned to each cores, *i.e.* CAWP tries to make the distribution of I-Page frames equal to each core. f_{ij} in (10) in Section 5.1 have priority of consideration in CAWP algorithm which can influence the result of (13) in Section 5.1.

Conflict-aware Assignment with Conflict Priority (CACP) Algorithm

In CACP algorithm, the number of bits of tag of each core is the key factor to decide which core can get the new I-Page frame. Similarly, the following steps give the description of CACP algorithm.

(1) Load a page of instructions into an I-Page frame whose page frame number is N.

(2) Find out which cores have the smallest number of bits of tag when I-Page frame N is assigned to all cores. If only one core is found, assign I-Page frame N to the core found; otherwise, go to Step 3.

(3) Check whether the core where I-Page frame N-1 was assigned is in the result of Step 2. If it is, assign I-Page frame N to the core where I-Page frame N-1 was assigned; otherwise assign I-Page frame N to random cores in the result.

(4) Reduce tag.

(5)   If more pages of instruction are needed to load into physical memory, return to Step 1; otherwise end.

CACP algorithm focuses on the number of bits of tag, *i.e.* CACP algorithm tries to decrease or avoid tag-reduction conflicts. $\overline{B_{ij}}$ in (7) in Section 5.1 have priority of consideration in CACP algorithm which can influence the result of (13) in Section 5.1.

Among the 3 algorithms, RANP algorithm only applies the tag reduction technique to the multi-core processor without any other optimization; CAWP algorithm applies the tag reduction with a optimization in which the number of I-Page frames assigned to cores have a priority to be considered: CACP algorithm also applies tag reduction but the number of bits of tags of cores have priority of consideration in optimization. CAWP and CACP algorithms optimize one of parameters of (13) in Section5.1, respectively.

Experiments and Results

Experiment Setup

The previous works of tag reduction on single-core processor [10, 11] only applies the tag reduction technique to the loop part of particular processes with help of operating system and compiler. The tag-reduction conflict gets worse as the number of page frames increases. Besides, the previous work used simulation in which only one thread is simulated. It is much different from the practical general operating system that is multi-process environment, so that the number of page frames and the possibility of tag-reduction conflict are different and much less than in real operating system.

The tag of VIPT I-Cache uses physical address. However, the physical address is decided by operating system and the usage of current physical memory. Operating system is a lazy system in which only when a page is needed, operating system then loads it into physical memory with page fault mechanism. And when a page frame is not used for a particular time, operating system will swap out this page to free the page frame. We cannot know which physical page frame a particular virtual page will use before this virtual page is loaded into physical memory. And details of how physical memory is used are the key to our method. As we want to get more precise results of energy saving by tag reduction on the multi-core processor, current simulation available cannot meet our request which needs to simulate the VIPT L1 caches, to implement the whole memory hierarchy, and to support to process schedule and page table functions provided by operating system. Most important, our method is much sensitive about the real-time usage of physical memory influenced by multi-process and multi-thread environment, so that we choose to collect the memory information we need from a real system.

Managing physical memory is one of the most important functions of operating system. We can probe the information of page frame distribution from operating system. We run and collect page frame information from benchmarks of SPEC2006 to make our experiment close to the real multi-process environment. Besides, our method applies tag reduction technique to the whole program rather than the loop part, so that compared to previous work on single-core processor that needs help of both compiler and operating system, our methodology only needs help of operating system.

Linux is open source, so it is easy for us to get information of page frame distribution by probing page table and other kernel components. We modified the Linux kernel and further added several modules developed by ourselves in order to collect the physical memory information we needed from Linux. As there is no difference in physical memory management of Linux between single core and multi-core processors, we can use the physical memory information collected from our experiment platform to get results of tag reduction in single-core or multi-core processors. Therefore, with the data we collected, we construct a scalable multi-core processor environment with that the maximum number of core supported is 8 to calculate the energy savings. Our experiment environment is listed in Table **1**.

Experimental Energy Saving Analysis

We use 23 benchmarks, including astar, bwaves, gromacs, cactusADM, bzip2, mcf, calculix, gcc, dealII, perlbench, GemsFDTD, zeusmp, h264ref, hmmer, lbm, libquantum, namd, povray, sjeng, soplex, tonto and Xalan from SPEC

CPU2006 benchmarks. Three copies of each benchmark are run concurrently every time to create a multi-process environment. Then we collect the experi-mental data from these 3 copies of each benchmark.

Figs. **5** and **6** show the energy consumption of the tag of each benchmark using five algorithms including No Tag reduction used (No Tag), Single-Core Tag Reduction (SCTR), RANP, CAWP and CACP. RANP, CAWP and CACP are algorithms for TRoCMP; and SCTR is the tag reduction on single-core processor proposed by previous work. No Tag is the one without any energy-saving optimization. In these experiments, the 4-core multi-core processor is used to evaluate these algorithms.

Table 1: Experiment Environment

OS Specification	Linux 2.6.11 32bit without PAE
Processor Model	Intel Core2 6400@2.13GHz
Physical Memory	1GB
Benchmark	SPEC CPU2006

As the range of energy consumption of benchmarks varies largely, with each benchmark, we compare algorithms to No Tag, using percentage to represent the energy consumption with each algorithm. Therefore, the range of Y-axis is from 0% to 100% and No Tag is always 100%, as No Tag compares to itself.

From Figs. **5** and **6**, we can find out that the RANP, CAWP and CACP consume less energy than No Tag and SCTR. In average, SCTR saves 49.43% energy, RANP saves 67.57%, CAWP saves 68.41% and CACP which is the best saves up to 76.16% energy.

Furthermore, if we concentrate on RANP, CAWP and CACP, with the result of every benchmark, we cannot judge easily which one is better between RANP and CAWP. Even with exact numbers above, they are still so close. It implies that making I-Page frames distribution equal to cores is not critical factor influencing the effect of the tag reduction. On the contrary, it affects the energy saving of tag reduction much to avoid the tag-reduction conflicts.

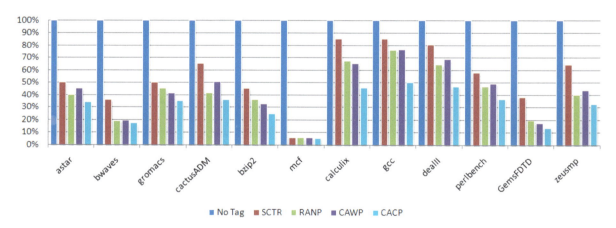

Figure 5: Comparison of energy consumption among different algorithms.

Figs. **7** and **8** show the energy consumption of the tag using CACP algorithm on variable number of cores. CACP-2, CACP-4 and CACP-8 represent using CACP algorithm on the 2-core, 4-core and 8-core processor, respectively.

Based on the analysis in Section 4, theoretically, the more number of cores, the less probability of the tag-reduction conflict occurs, and the less number of I-Page frames are assigned to each cores. Therefore, as the number of cores in-creases, the energy used by the tag should decrease. And the experiment results illustrated by Figs. **7** and **8** prove our theory. In average, CACP-2 saves 65.95% energy; CACP-4 saves 76.16% and CACP-8 saves up to 83.93%.

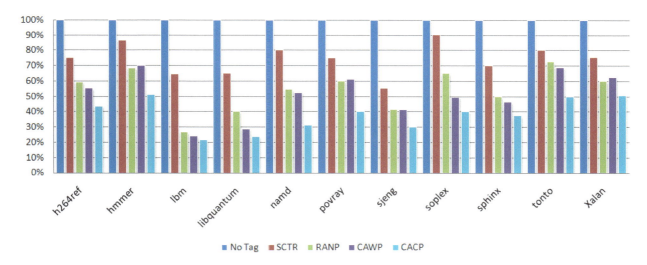

Figure 6: Comparison of energy consumption among different algorithms (Cont'd).

We also want to analyze the number of bits of the tag needed of each core using CAWP algorithm, since CAWP algorithm always make effort to keep the number of I-Page frames equal among cores; on the other hand, we analyze the number of I-Pages assigned to each core using CACP algorithm as well, since CACP algorithm always balances the length of each core's tag. With the two more analysis, we can get some deep conclusions of these algorithms. In this part, we use benchmark gcc, and execute 10 copies of this benchmark. In Figs. **9** and **10**, the x-axis is the time that benchmark run from start to end. And the number of bits and the number of I-Page frames are all 0 when the first copy of benchmark starts and all copies of benchmark have finished. These 0s are just omitted in Figs. **9** and **10**.

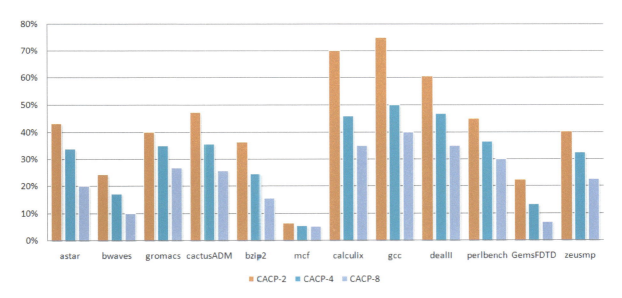

Figure 7: Energy consumption of 2-core, 4-core and 8-core processor using CACP algorithm.

Fig. **9** illustrates the number of bits of tag in each core, when CAWP algorithm is used. In this figure CAWP1 to CAWP4 represent Core 1 to Core 4 using CAWP algorithm. The difference in the number of bits of tag of each core from Core 1 to Core 4 is fairly big from this figure. As the number of physical page frames assigned to each cores have priority to consider in CAWP, CAWP algorithm always make the number of physical page frames balance on each core, but it does not avoid the tag reduction conflict. The number of bits of tag of each core can influence the energy consumption, according to (13) in section 5.1. This is the reason why the effect of energy saving of CAWP cannot be improved more than RANP.

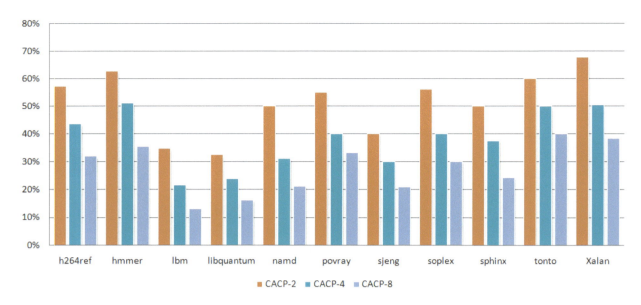

Figure 8: Energy consumption of 2-core, 4-core and 8-core processor using CACP algorithm (Cont'd).

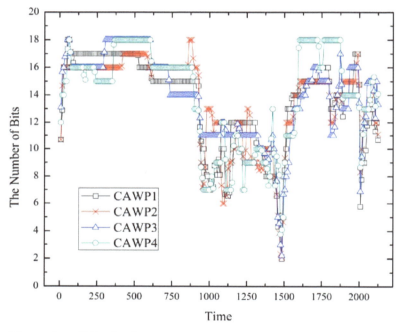

Figure 9: Comparison of the number of bits of each core.

Fig. **10** shows the number of I-Page frames assigned to each core, when CACP algorithm is used. CACP1 to CACP4 indicate Core 1 to Core 4 with CACP algorithm. CACP is designed to keep the number of bits of tag balance in each core, but does not take account the number of I-Page frames of each core. CACP saves energy most, nonetheless, the workload of each core is not balance.

TROCMP WITH CONSTRAINT OF PERFORMANCE OVERHEAD

Core Degree and Performance Overhead

Based on the analysis in Section 4, TRoCMP can exploit more opportunities to gain more energy saving than the one on a single-core processor by assigning page frames to different cores. In practice, TRoCMP divides the whole page frames of each thread into several parts to de-crease or avoid the tag-reduction conflicts. The Core Degree is thus introduced here to represent the number of cores that the page frames of a thread can be assigned to. The minimal Core Degree is 1 and the maximal is equal to the total number of cores. The Core Degree equal to 1 means that all the page frames of each thread are assigned to one particular core. On the contrary, if Core Degree is equal to the number of cores, it means that page frames of each thread are assigned to all cores. The larger the value of Core Degree is, the more cores the page frames of each thread can be distributed to. In theory, a larger value of Core Degree provides opportunities to avoid tag-reduction conflicts, and at the same time, allows less number of page frames in average to be assigned to each core decreases. Both are beneficial to the energy savings.

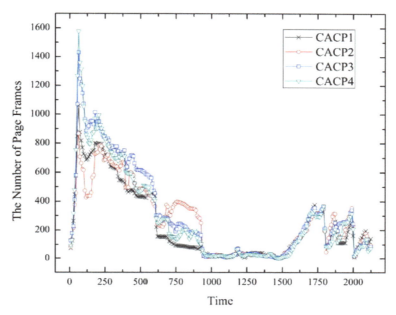

Figure 10: Comparison of the number of the I-Page assigned to each core.

Recall that tag reduction needs page frames of each thread to be divided into parts. We consider each part as non-parallel, as the data dependency between parts may exist. And each non-parallel part is designed to be treated as a thread by operating system. The number of non-parallel parts depends on the decision of tag reduction on multi-core processor. Because the concurrency of threads still remains, the non-parallel parts of different threads can run on different cores simultaneously. Besides, these non-parallel parts also follow the affiliation mechanism of operating system, that is, each non-parallel part is always executed on the core that it is originally distributed to by operating system. Now, Equation (3) can be refined as where N_{ij} is the number of page frames of the *j-th* parts on core i, p_i is the number of parts on core i, d is the number of cores that have the parts and σ is the value of Core Degree.

$$\begin{cases} B_{cmp}^i = \log_2 \sum_{j=1}^{p_i} N_{ij} \\ N = \sum_{i=1}^{d} \sum_{j=1}^{p_i} N_{ij}, d \leq \sigma \end{cases} \tag{14}$$

Although TRoCMP does not break the concurrency of threads, the non-parallel parts lead to extra thread switches. The thread switch takes system time, so the extra thread switches slow down the system. This is the performance overhead induced by tag reduction on multi-core processor. Therefore, as the value of Core Degree goes up, the extra thread switches increases and then the performance of system goes down.

In a word, the Core Degree used by tag reduction on multi-core processor effects both energy saving and the overhead of performance. When it grows, tag reduction can save more energy of multi-core processor but causes more performance overhead. The balance of energy saving and performance overhead is determined by Core Degree.

Refined Energy Consumption and Heuristic Algorithm

In this section, we first refine energy consumption of TRoCMP with the Core Degree constraint, then propose an extensive algorithm to implement the Core Degree, based on CACP algorithm that is the best algorithm of our proposed 3 algorithms in Section 5.2.

With the constraint of Core Degree, (4) has to be added a formula to represent Core Degree constraint. Therefore, (4) can be extended as

$$E = e \cdot \sum_{i=1}^{s} \sum_{j=1}^{w} \sum_{n=1}^{a_{ij}} TagR(\bigcup_{m=1}^{t} AddEx(I_{ij}(m,n))), \tag{15}$$

subject to $\forall i, 1 \leq i \leq s$, $\forall m, 1 \leq m \leq t$, and $\forall n, 1 \leq n \leq a_{ij}$

$$\sigma \geq w - \sum_{j=1}^{w} \phi(I_{ij}(m,n)). \tag{16}$$

Equation (16) guarantees that instructions of each thread can be only assigned to at most σ number of cores, due to the Core Degree constraint. It is formulated by the function $\phi(S)$ which returns 1 if set S is a empty set or 0 otherwise. So, (13) can be extended as

$$\begin{cases} E \leq \mathcal{E} = e \cdot N_{max} \cdot \sum_{i=1}^{s} \sum_{j=1}^{w} (\overline{B_{ij}} \cdot f_{ij}) \\ \sigma \geq w - \sum_{j=1}^{w} \phi(I_{ij}(m,n)) \end{cases} \tag{17}$$

For loading instruction pages of Thread M, the refined heuristic algorithm based on CACP algorithm can be described concisely as follows.

(1) Load a page of instructions that is part of Thread M into an I-Page frame with page frame number N.

(2) If the number of cores that the I-Page frames of Thread M have been assigned to is less than Core Degree, then go to step 3; otherwise go to step 4.

(3) In all cores, find out the one with the shortest reduced tag if the N-th I-Page frame is included; then go to Step 5.

(4) Within the cores that Thread M has already been assigned to, find out the one with the shortest reduced tag if the N-th I-Page frame is included.

(5) Dispatch the I-Page frame to the chosen core and make tag reduction.

(6) If more pages of instructions of Thread M need to be loaded into physical memory, return to Step 1; otherwise terminate.

Because this algorithm is based on CACP, it incorporates the affiliation mechanism and implements TRoCMP under a given Core Degree. As shown in the analysis above, the effect of TRoCMP depends on the number of page frames of each core and the probability of tag-reduction conflicts. Since the tag-reduction conflict is always more crucial than the other, we consider it as the priority factor to design this heuristic algorithm. That is, we try to decrease and avoid the tag-reduction conflicts as much as possible in this algorithm.

Performance Overhead and Trade-off Analysis of TRoCMP

Performance Overhead Analysis

To formulate the discussion in Section 6.1, the performance overhead is defined as the number of the additional thread switches induced by tag reduction. We first show the total number of switches, ST, on a tag reduction enabled multi-core processor as

$$ST = SP + SR - \varepsilon, \varepsilon \ll SP, SR \qquad (18)$$

where SP is the number of thread switches when no tag reduction is not used, SR is the number of thread switches caused by the additional non-parallel parts, and ε is the overlap between SP and SR. Generally, the overlap rarely happens, only in some very special cases, for example, when a thread switch caused by additional non-parallel parts should have occurred because of the expiration of time slice of operating system. So ε is far less than SP or SR. The performance overhead caused by TRoCMP T is

$$T = SR - \varepsilon \qquad (19)$$

Similar to (4), for a multi-core processor with w cores and t running threads, SR in a period with s time slices can be calculated as

$$SR = \sum_{m=1}^{t} \sum_{i=1}^{s} \frac{F_{im} - 1}{P_{im}} \sum_{j=1}^{w} a_{ij}, \qquad (20)$$

subject to $\forall i, 1 \le i \le s$ and $\forall m, 1 \le m \le t$

$$F_{im} \le \sigma. \qquad (21)$$

In (20) P_{im} is the number of I-Pages of the *m-th* thread during the *i-th* time slice, F_{im} is the number of non-parallel threads that are generated by the *m-th* thread during the *i-th* time slice; and the definition of a_{ij} is the same as in (6). Due to the core-degree constraint, F_{im} must not exceed σ, which is described by (21).

Similarly, using N_i defined in (9), we can simplify (20) as

$$SR = \sum_{m=1}^{t} \sum_{i=1}^{s} \frac{N_i}{P_{im}}(F_{im} - 1) \qquad (22)$$

So, T can be expressed as

$$T = \sum_{m=1}^{t} \sum_{i=1}^{s} (N_i \cdot (F_{im} - 1)/P_{im}) - \varepsilon \qquad (23)$$

The upper bound of the performance overhead T caused by extra non-parallel parts when tag reduction applied to multi-core processor can eventually be derived as

$$\begin{cases} T \le \mathcal{T} = N_{max} \cdot \sum\limits_{m=1}^{t} \sum\limits_{i=1}^{s} ((F_{im} - 1)/P_{im}) \\ F_{im} \le \sigma \end{cases} \qquad (24)$$

We notice that, $\mathcal{T}$ only related to F_{im} and P_{im}, since N_{max} and SP are constants for each thread. When the tag reduction is not used, that is, F_{im} is always equal to 1, $\mathcal{T}$ is equal to 0, as expected.

Energy and Performance Trade-off Analysis

In order to facilitate the comparison of the energy consumption and performance overhead under various Core Degrees for a group of applications, we introduce the normalized metrics θ and ω as follows.

$$\theta_n^\sigma = \mathcal{E}_n^\sigma / \mathcal{E}_n^{\sigma^{min}}, \theta_n^\sigma \in (0, 1] \qquad (25)$$

and

$$\omega_n^\sigma = \mathcal{T}_n^\sigma / \mathcal{T}_n^{\sigma^{max}}, \omega_n^\sigma \in (0, 1] \tag{26}$$

in which θ_n^σ is the ratio of energy consumption of the *n-th* application when Core Degree is equal to σ relative to the one when Core Degree is σ^{min}, and ω_n^σ is the ratio of performance overhead of the *n-th* application when Core Degree is set to σ relative to the one when Core Degree is σ^{max}. As we apply TRoCMP, the minimal value of Core Degree σ^{min} is 2. The maximal value of Core Degree σ^{max} is equal to the number of cores. Similarly, $\mathcal{E}_n^\sigma$ and $\mathcal{T}_n^\sigma$ represent the energy consumption and performance overhead of the *n-th* application, respectively, when Core Degree is equal to σ. Based on our analysis, as Core Degree σ increases, θ_n^σ goes down from 1, and ω_n^σ goes up to 1.

Theoretically, the energy consumption always decreases and the performance overhead always increases as Core Degree varies from 2 to the number of cores. It is meaningless that compare the energy consumption and performance overhead directly. Instead, we could compare the trends of energy consumption with the one of performance overhead of different applications as Core Degree varies to find out the trade-off of the energy and performance of TRoCMP. So the trend of energy consumption and performance overhead, can be calculated as

$$\eta_n(\sigma) = -\frac{d\theta_n}{d\sigma}, \sigma \in (\sigma^{min}, +\infty) \tag{27}$$

and

$$\gamma_n(\sigma) = \frac{d\omega_n}{d\sigma}, \sigma \in (\sigma^{min}, +\infty) \tag{28}$$

where η and γ are the trends of energy consumption and performance overhead of the *n-th* application, respectively. Equation (27) makes sure that the trend of energy consumption η is positive to compare with γ, since energy consumption usually goes down as Core Degree increases so that the value of $\frac{d\theta_n}{d\sigma}$ is negative.

So far, we can use the trends of energy consumption and performance overhead to find out the appropriate value of Core Degree. In microprocessor design, it is demanded to consume less energy with low performance cost. However, with TRoCMP, the energy consumption always goes down and the performance overhead always goes up, so that with a particular value of Core Degree, the bigger the value of η_n is and the less the value of γ_n is, the better the Core Degree is. Therefore, the appropriate value of Core Degree of each application can be determined as follows:

$$\sigma_n = \begin{cases} \arg\min_\sigma(|\gamma_n(\sigma) - \eta_n(\sigma)|) & : & \text{Case 1} \\ \arg\min_\sigma(\gamma_n(\sigma) - \eta_n(\sigma)) & : & \text{Case 2} \\ any \in [\sigma^{min}, \sigma^{max}] & : & \text{Case 3} \\ \arg\min_\sigma(\gamma_n(\sigma) - \eta_n(\sigma)) & : & else \end{cases} \tag{29}$$

where Case 1, 2, 3 can be expressed as follows.

Case 1:

$$\eta_n(\sigma^{min} + \Delta) > \gamma_n(\sigma^{min} + \Delta) \text{ and}$$
$$\exists \sigma' \in (\sigma^{min}, +\infty), \eta_n(\sigma') = \gamma_n(\sigma')$$

Case 2:

$$\eta_n(\sigma^{min} + \Delta) < \gamma_n(\sigma^{min} + \Delta) \text{ and}$$
$$\exists m' \in (\sigma^{min}, +\infty), \eta_n(m') = \gamma_m(m')$$

Case 3:

$$\eta_n(\sigma) \equiv \gamma_n(\sigma) + C,$$
C is a constant number.

In (29), σ_n is the appropriate value of Core Degree of the *n-th* application. There are 3 situations when we decide the best value of Core Degree described in the equation above. If we can find a common value of σ_n for sorts of applications, we can know the best value of Core Degree that achieve the trade-off of the energy consumption and performance overhead of tag reduction on multi-core processor.

Experiments and Results

In our experiment, we use 22 benchmarks from SPEC CPU2006 to find out the appropriate value of Core Degree, as the benchmarks from SPEC CPU2006 represent sorts of classic applications. Firstly, we construct an experiment platform to evaluate 22 benchmarks and collect necessary data; then we calculate the energy consumption, performance overhead and their trend as described above; finally, the appropriate value of Core Degree can be got through the ones of 22 benchmarks.

Experiment Setup

Similar to the last experiments, we still choose Linux as our experiment platform. And we modify the Linux kernel and add some modules to collect experimental data. The details of experiment environment are the same as the one shown in Table **1**. In this experiment, we construct a 16-core multi-core environment to calculate energy consumption and performance overhead with varying of Core Degree, such that we can find the optimal value of Core Degree.

The names of 22 benchmarks evaluated are listed in Table **2** alphabetically. And we will use the index of each benchmark instead of using its name for convenience. The benchmarks consist of integer and float computation. Since in our experiments, we apply the tag reduction on a 16-core processor, the range of Core Degree is from 2 to 16, *i.e.* σ^{min} and σ^{max} are 2 and 16, respectively. We evaluate each of 22 benchmarks with different values of Core Degree from 2 to 16 with interval by 2.

Table 2: The benchmark List

Index	1	2	3	4
Name	astar	bwaves	bzip2	cactusADM
Index	5	6	7	8
Name	calculix	dealII	gcc	GemsFDTD
Index	9	10	11	12
Name	gromacs	h264ref	hmmer	lbm
Index	13	14	15	16
Name	libquantum	namd	perlbench	povray
Index	17	18	19	20
Name	sjeng	soplex	sphinx	tonto
Index	21	22		
Name	Xalan	zeusmp		

Experiment Result and Analysis

Based on the analysis in Section 6.3, with the data collected from our experiment platform, we can calculate θ_n^m and ω_n^m that are en-ergy consumption ratio and performance overhead ratio of each benchmark when Core Degree varies, where n is from 1 to 2 and m is from 2 to 16 with interval by 2.

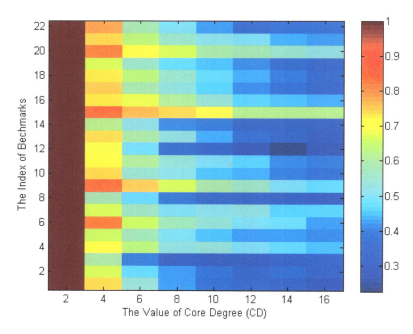

Figure 11: The discrete results of energy con-sumption as Core Degree varies.

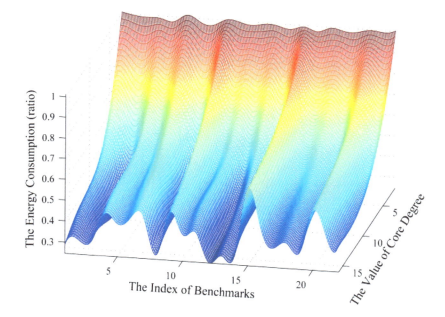

Figure 12: The fitted results of energy consumption as Core Degree varies.

Fig. **11** illustrates the energy consumption ratio of each benchmark when Core Degree is equal to 2, 4, till 16. The values of ratio are distributed discretely by the discrete values of Core Degree, because the original experimental results are discrete. The x-axis is the value of Core Degree, and the y-axis is the index of benchmarks. Different colors in Fig. **11** represent the values of energy consumption, which is shown in the color bar on the right in details. Each row shows the energy consumption of each benchmark as Core Degree varies. With Fig. **11** we can find out that the energy of consumption of all the benchmarks decreases when the value of Core Degree increases. And the value of energy consumption of all benchmarks is 1 when Core Degree is 2, which is implied by the first column in this figure. The results illustrated in Fig. **11** and the theoretical analysis in Section 6.1 fit neatly.

The energy consumption ratio is fitted, with help of Matlab, so that the energy consumption ratio of each benchmark varies consecutively along the value of Core Degree, which is depicted in Fig. **12**. In this figure, the x-axis is the value of Core Degree, y-axis is the index of benchmarks, and z-axis is the ratio of energy consumption. This figure smoothes the results in Fig. **11** and offers us a global view of energy consumption of all benchmarks along values of Core Degree. From Fig. **12**, we can see that the differences in energy consumption of all benchmarks is bigger and bigger as the value of Core Degree varies from 2 to 16. Furthermore, it is obvious to find out that the energy consumption decreases fast when the value of Core Degree is small, but turns more and more slowly when the value of Core Degree becomes bigger. Therefore, the effect of energy saving is weaker as the value of Core Degree increases.

Figs. **13** and **14** depict the performance overhead ratio of each benchmark with different values of Core Degree. Similar to Figs. **11** and **12**, the results shown in Fig. **13** is original and discrete and the one in Fig. **14** is fitted and successive.

In Fig. **13**, although the last column implies that the performance overhead ratio of all benchmarks is 1 when the value of Core Degree is 16, we notice that the maximum of color bar on the right achieve more than 1.2. The results of performance overhead ratio of Most of 22 benchmarks are monotonic increment along the varying of Core Degree from 2 to 16. However, some benchmarks behave more complicatedly than monotonity, such as No. 4, No. 7, No 10, No 11 and No 15 benchmark. The results of performance overhead ratio from experiments are a bit more complex than the theory in Section 6.1.

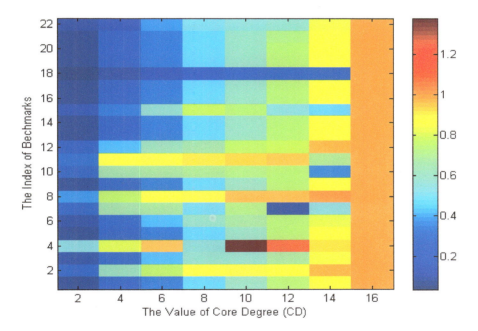

Figure 13: The discrete results of performance cost as Core Degree varies.

The fitted results of performance overhead ratio illustrated by Fig. **14** make the varying of performance overhead ratio of each benchmark with different values of Core Degree more clearly. In Fig. **14**, the x-axis is the value of Core Degree, the y-axis is the index of benchmarks, and the z-axis is the performance overhead ratio. Except for fluctuating of some bench-marks, the performance overhead ratio almost increases as the value of Core Degree goes up. From Fig. **14**, we can also find out the non-monotonity of some benchmarks, as well.

The results of energy consumption and performance overhead are illustrated by Figs. **11** to **14**. With the results above, we should follow the analysis in Section 6.3 to get the trends of energy consumption and performance overhead of each bench-mark, η_n and γ_n, respectively. This is basis of determine the appropriate value of Core Degree. The trends are calculated by derivative, which needs both the energy consumption ratio and the performance overhead ratio are consecutive or can be expressed by equations. Whereas, the re-sults we get from our platform are discrete because of the discrete value of Core Degree from 2 to 16 with interval by 2.

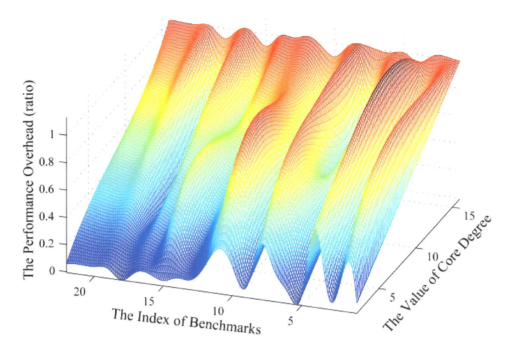

Figure 14: The fitted results of performance cost as Core Degree varies.

In order to get η_n and γ_n, we fit the energy consumption ratio function and performance overhead ratio function with the their discrete results with help of Matlab. With the functions fitted, we can get the expressions of derivative of these functions, so that the trends are available for calculation.

Before showing results of derivative of fitted ratio, we will present the original discrete results first. Instead of using $-\frac{d\theta_n}{dm}$ and $\frac{d\omega_n}{dm}$ to calculate the η_n and γ_n, respectively, we adopt the following equations to get the original discrete results.

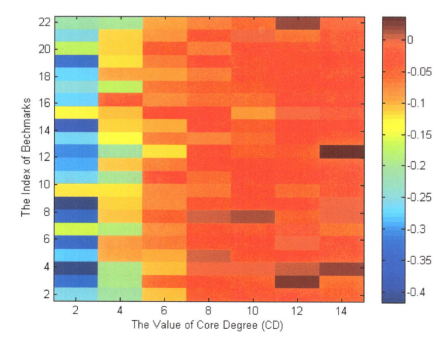

Figure 15: The discrete results of differential of energy consumption as Core Degree varies.

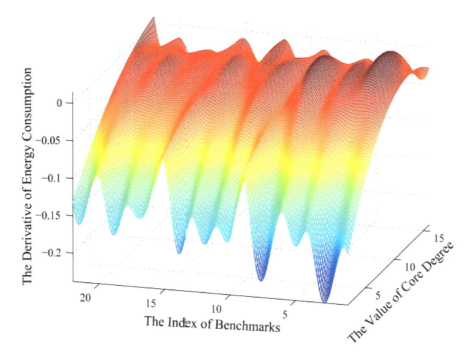

Figure 16: The results of derivative of fitted energy consumption as Core Degree varies.

$$\eta'_n(m) = (\theta_n^{m+2} - \theta_n^m) \tag{30}$$

and

$$\gamma'_n(m) = (\omega_n^{m+2} - \omega_n^m) \tag{31}$$

where $\eta'_n(m)$ and $\gamma'_n(m)$ are the discrete results of differential of the energy consumption and performance overhead of each benchmark when using discrete value of Core Degree.

Fig. **15** shows the discrete results of differential of the energy consumption. The x-axis is the value of m in (30) and y-axis is the index of benchmarks. The results of differential of energy consumption trends to 0 along the varying of m from 2 to 14, which implies that the effect of energy saving by TRoCMP is weaker and weaker when Core Degree varies incrementally.

Fig. **16** shows the results of derivative of fitted energy consumption ratio of each benchmark when Core Degree varies consecutively. The x-axis is the value of Core Degree, the y-axis is the index of benchmarks and z-axis is the derivative of energy consumption ratio. It is noticed that the value of z-axis is $-\eta_n(m) = \frac{d\theta_n}{dm}$ rather than (27), since the energy consumption is less and less as the value of Core Degree varies incrementally. From Fig. **16**, we find out that the results of derivative of fitted energy consumption ratio vary similarly among all benchmarks. And when Core Degree is greater than 12, the results of derivative of fitted energy consumption ratio of part of benchmarks achieve their peaks, the one of others then still remain monotonic, which means after Core Degree is 12, part of benchmarks can save more energy, and the others are otherwise.

Similar to Figs. **15** and **16**, Figs. **17** and **18** depict the trend of performance overhead of each benchmark with different values of Core Degree. The discrete results of differential of the performance overhead ratio are shown in Fig. **17**. The x-axis is the value of m in (31), the y-axis is the index of benchmarks. We notice that the trends of most of benchmarks remain stable; the ones of others are otherwise. Besides, the minimal value of the color bar is negative, and the negative values appear several times in the this figure, which means the performance overhead decreases when Core Degree is equal to some particular values.

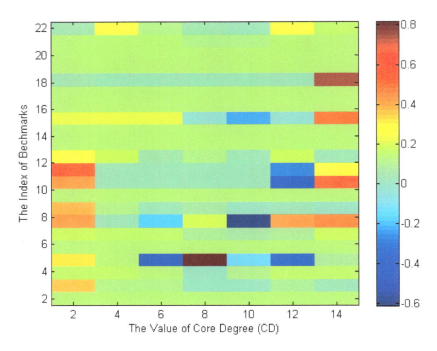

Figure 17: The discrete results of differential of performance overhead as Core Degree varies.

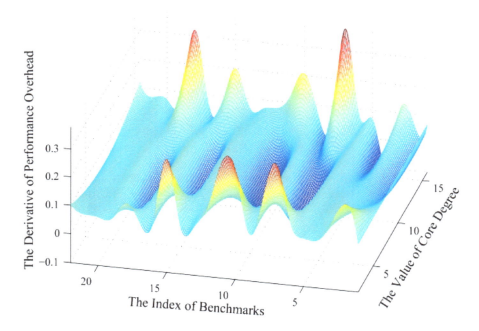

Figure 18: The results of derivative of fitted performance overhead as Core Degree varies.

Fig. **18** that depicts the results of derivative of the fitted performance over-head ratio gives us a more clear view of the trends of performance overhead of all benchmarks with consecutive Core Degree. The x-axis is the value of Core Degree, the y-axis is the index of benchmarks and z-axis is the results of derivative of performance overhead ratio. It is obvious that all benchmarks can be divided into two parts: Part A and Part B. The derivative of performance overhead ratio of benchmarks in Part A stays almost the same; on the contrary the one in Part B changes dramatically as the value of Core Degree varies. By observing the bench-marks in latter part, it is found that their shapes are like bow-the the results of derivative are high when Core Degree is at both ends of its range, and the one are low when Core Degree is at middle part of its range. With further observation, the negative values in Fig. **17** all appear in the benchmarks belong to Part B.

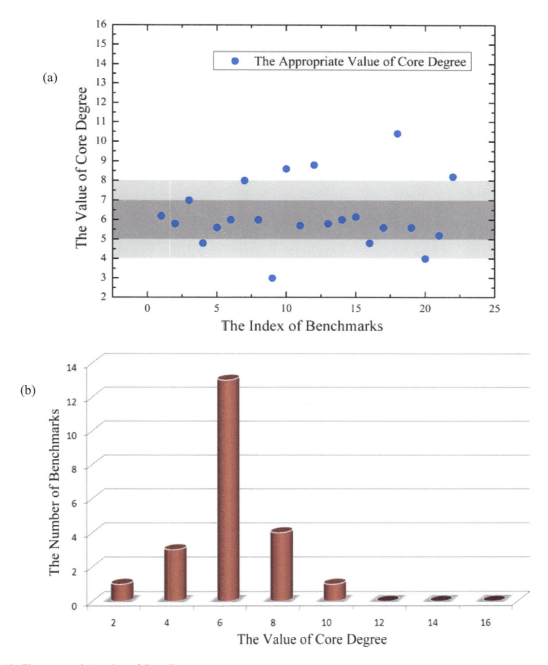

Figure 19: The appropriate value of Core Degree

Now, with the results of derivative of the fitted energy consumption ration and performance overhead of each benchmark as the value Core Degree varies successively, we can get the appropriate value of Core Degree of each benchmark, *i.e.* σ_n, according the (29) in Section 6.3. The distribution of σ_n is illustrated in Fig. **19(a)**. Each point in this figure shows a particular benchmark's appropriate value of Core Degree. The x-value of a point is the index of a benchmark, and the y-value of the point is the appropriate value of Core Degree of this benchmark. There are two districts in this figure. One is the filled with light grey and the other is with dark grey. The light grey district is a district around Core Degree 6 with radius 2; and the dark grey district is a district around Core Degree 6 with radius

1. The appropriate values of Core Degree of 22 benchmarks are distributed between 3 and 10. Most of benchmarks are in light grey district, especially in dark grey district. Fig. **19(b)** offers the distribution with number more clearly. In this figure, the x-axis is the value of Core Degree; the y-axis is the number of Benchmarks. Taking the cylinder at Core Degree 6 for example, this cylinder represents that the appropriate values of 13 benchmarks is in the interval of (5,7]. Therefore, we can see that all appropriate values of Core Degree of benchmarks are from 2 to 10, with a peak at Core Degree 6 that is much higher than ones at other Core Degree. As the benchmarks from SPEC CPU2006 represent sorts of typical application, from the results in Fig. **19**, we can find out when Core Degree is 6, it is appropriate for application to make trade-off of energy consumption and performance overhead.

CONCLUSIONS

In this chapter, we overview the research on a multi-core processor and energy saving. The fundamental of energy saving achieved by tag reduction is presented and analyzed. Furthermore, we propose a novel method TRoCMP that uses tag reduction on a multi-core processor.

TRoCMP can be used to evaluate the algorithms to find out how to reduce tag in L1 I-Cache on the multi-core processor and reduce tag more with multi-core architecture's characteristics. We formulate our approach to an equivalent problem which is to find an assignment of the whole instruction pages in the physical memory to a set of cores such that the tag-reduction conflicts for each core can be mostly avoided or reduced. Then three algorithms, RANP Algorithm, CAWP Algorithm, and CACP Algorithm are pro-posed using different heuristics for this assignment problem.

After the analysis of energy saving of TRoCMP, we analyze the performance overhead caused by TRoCMP, and then introduce the Core Degree mechanism to balance the energy consumption and performance cost. Furthermore the analysis of energy and performance trade-offs lead to finding out an appropriate Core Degree.

In the experiments, we modify the Linux kernel to collect adequate experimental data from a real Linux system. Finally, with the results of experiment and calculation, we find out that the best algorithm CACP saves up to 76.16% and 83.93% energy, on 4-core and 8-core multi-core processor respectively, com-pared to the case in which no tag re-duction is used. Also, our results show a great potential in energy saving using tag reduction technique than SCTR.

And considering performance overhead, we use 22 benchmarks of SPEC CPU2006 to evaluate TRoCMP and to find out the optimal value of Core Degree. The experimental results show that when the Core Degree is 6, we can get the most desired trade-off of energy saving and performance cost.

From view of energy saving and performance overhead, TRoCMP can save much energy of L1 I-Cache of multi-core processors, and it can keep the performance overhead in a reasonable boundary with the Core Degree mechanism.

ACKNOWLEDGEMENTS

This work is supported by Fellowships of the Japan Society for the Promotion of Science for Young Scientists Program, Excellent Young Researcher Overseas Visit Program, National 973 Basic Research Program of China under grant No. 2007CB310900, and National Natural Science Foundation of China under Grant Nos. 60725208, 60811130528.

The authors are deeply grateful to Dr. Feilong Tang, and Mr. Zhuo Li at the University of Aizu, and Dr. Xuping Tu in the Services Computing Technology and System Lab at Huazhong University of Science and Technology.

REFERENCES

[1]   L. Spracklen and S. Abraham, "Chip multithreading: Opportunities and challenges," in Proceedings of the 11th International Symposium on High-Performance Computer Architecture. IEEE Computer Society Washington, DC, USA, 2005, pp. 248–252.

[2]   J. Held, J. Bautista, and S. Koehl, "From a few cores to many: A tera-scale computing research overview," Research at Intel white paper, 2006.

[3]   E. Lindholm, J. Nickolls, S. Oberman, and J. Montrym, "NVIDIA Tesla: A unified graphics and computing architecture," IEEE Micro, pp. 39–55, 2008.

[4]   M. Monchiero, G. Palermo, C. Silvano, and O. Villa, "Efficient synchronization for embedded on-chip multiprocessors," vol. 14, no. 10, pp. 1049–1062, 2006.

[5]   J. Edmondson, P. Rubinfeld, P. Bannon, B. Benschneider, D. Bernstein, R. Castelino, E. Cooper, D. Dever, D. Donchin, T. Fischer *et al.*, "Internal organization of the Alpha 21164, a 300-MHz 64-bit quad-issue CMOS RISC microprocessor," Digital Technical Journal, vol. 7, no. 1, pp. 119–135, 1995.

[6]   J. Montanaro, R. Witek, K. Anne, A. Black, E. Cooper, D. Dobberpuhl, P. Donahue, J. Eno, W. Hoeppner, D. Kruckemyer *et al.*, "A 160-mhz, 32-b, 0.5-w CMOS RISC microprocessor," IEEE Journal of Solid-State Circuits, vol. 31, no. 11, pp. 1703–1714, 1996.

[7]   J. Henning, "SPEC CPU2006 benchmark descriptions," ACM SIGARCH Computer Architecture News, vol. 34, no. 4, p. 17, 2006.

[8]   P. Petrov and A. Orailoglu, "Dynamic tag reduction for low-power caches in embedded systems with virtual memory," International Journal of Parallel Programming, vol. 35, no. 2, pp. 157–177, 2007.

[9]   P. P. and O. A., "Virtual page tag reduction for low-power TLBs," in 21st International Conference on Computer Design, 2003. Proceedings, 2003, pp. 371–374.

[10]   X. Zhou and P. Petrov, "Heterogeneously Tagged Caches for Low-Power Embedded Systems with Virtual Memory Support," ACM transactions on design automation of electronic systems, vol. 13, no. 2, p. 32, 2008.

[11]   P. Petrov and A. Orailoglu, "Tag compression for low power in dynamically customizable embedded processors," IEEE Transactions on Computer-Aided Design of Integrated Circuits and Systems, vol. 23, no. 7, pp. 1031–1047, 2004.

[12]   K. Inoue, T. Ishihara, and K. Murakami, "Way-predicting set-associative cache for high performance and low energy consumption," in Proceedings of the 1999 international symposium on Low power electronics and design. ACM, 1999, p. 275.

[13]   C. McNairy and D. Soltis, "Itanium 2 processor microarchitecture," IEEE Micro, vol. 23, no. 2, pp. 44–55, 2003.

[14]   "MIPS R1000 Microprocessor User's Manual," in MIPS Technologies, Inc., 1996, p. version 2.0.

[15]   R. Kessler *et al.*, "The alpha 21264 microprocessor," IEEE micro, vol. 19, no. 2, pp. 24–36, 1999.

[16]   W. Tang, R. Gupta, A. Nicolau, and A. Veidenbaum, "Simultaneous way-footprint prediction and branch prediction for energy savings in set-associative instruction caches," in IEEE Workshop on Power Management for Real-Time and Embedded Systems. Citeseer, 2001.

[17]   A. Nicolaescu, "Low Energy, Highly-Associative Cache Design for Embedded Processors," in ICCD 2004: IEEE International Conference on Computer Design: VLSI in computers & processors: proceedings: 11-13 October, 2004, San Jose, CA. Institute of Electrical & Electronics Engineers (IEEE), 2004, p. 332.

[18]   M. Powell, S. Yang, B. Falsafi, K. Roy, T. N. Vijaykumar, "Gated-Vdd: a circuit technique to reduce leakage in deep-submicron cache memories", in Proceedings of the 2000 international symposium on Low power electronics and design, p.90-95, July 25-27, 2000, Rapallo, Italy.

[19]   D. Parikh, Y. Zhang, K. Sankaranarayanan, K. Skadron, and M. Stan, "Comparison of State-Preserving vs. Non-State-Preserving Leakage Control in Caches," in Workshop on Duplicating, Deconstructing and Debunking, vol. 226. Citeseer, 2003.

[20]   S. Kaxiras, Z. Hu, and M. Martonosi, "Cache decay: exploiting generational behavior to reduce cache leakage power," COMPUTER ARCHITECTURE NEWS, vol. 29, no. 2, pp. 240–253, 2001.

[21]   K. Flautner, N. Kim, S. Martin, D. Blaauw, and T. Mudge, "Drowsy caches: simple techniques for reducing leakage power," in Proceedings of the 29th annual international symposium on Computer architecture. IEEE Computer Society Washington, DC, USA, 2002, pp. 148–157.

[22]   S. Petit, J. Sahuquillo, J. Such, and D. Kaeli, 'Exploiting temporal locality in drowsy cache policies," in Proceedings of the 2nd conference on Computing frontiers. ACM New York, NY, USA, 2005, pp. 371–377.

[23]   E. Tam, J. Rivers, V. Srinivasan, G. Tyson, and E. Davidson, "Active management of data caches by exploiting reuse information," IEEE Transactions on Computers, vol. 48, no. 11, pp. 1244–1259, 1999.

[24]   C. Hsu and U. Kremer, "The design, implementation, and evaluation of a compiler algorithm for CPU energy reduction," in Proceedings of the ACM SIGPLAN 2003 conference on Programming language design and implementation. ACM New York, NY, USA, 2003, pp. 38–48.

[25]   Y. Chen, Z. Shao, Q. Zhuge, C. Xue, B. Xiac, and H. Edwin, "Minimizing Energy *via* Loop Scheduling and DVS for Multi-Core Embedded Systems," in Proceedings of the 11th International Conference on Parallel and Distributed Systems-Workshops (ICPADS'05)-Volume 02. IEEE Computer Society Washington, DC, USA, 2005, pp. 2–6.

[26]   J. Shirako, N. Oshiyama, Y. Wada, and H. Shikano, "Compiler Control Power Saving Scheme for Multi Core Processors," in Languages and Compilers for Parallel Computing: 18th International Workshop, LCPC 2005, Hawthorne, NY, USA, October 20-22, 2005: Revised Selected Papers. Springer Verlag, 2006, p. 362.

[27]   R. Inc, "Rambus 128/144-Mbit Direct RDRAM Data Sheet," 2000.

[28]   V. Delaluz, A. Sivasubramaniam, M. Kandemir, N. Vijaykrishnan, and M. Irwin, "Scheduler-based DRAM energy management," in Proceedings of the 39th conference on Design automation. ACM New York, NY, USA, 2002, pp. 697–702.

[29]   V. Delaluz, M. Kandemir, N. Vijaykrishnan, A. Sivasubramaniam, and M. Irwin, "DRAM energy management using software and hardware directed powermode control," in The Seventh International Symposium on High-Performance Computer Architecture, 2001. HPCA., 2001, pp. 159–169.

[30]   V. Delaluz, M. Kandemir, N. Vijaykrishnan, A. Sivasubramaniam, and M. Irwin, "Hardware and software techniques for controlling dram power modes," IEEE Transactions on Computers, pp. 1154–1173, 2001.

CHAPTER 4

Model-Driven Multi-core Embedded Software Design

Chao-Sheng Lin[1], Pao-Ann Hsiung[1], Chih-Hung Chang[2], Nien-Lin Hsueh[3], Chorng-Shiuh Koong[4], Chih-Hsiong Shih[5], Chao-Tung Yang[5], and William C.-C. Chu[5]

[1]*National Chung Cheng University, Chiayi, Taiwan;* [2]*Hsiuping Institute of Technology, Taichung, Taiwan;* [3]*Feng Chia University, Taichung, Taiwan;* [4]*National Taichung University, Taichung, Taiwan and* [5]*Tunghai University, Taichung, Taiwan*

Abstract: Multi-core processors have emerged rapidly in personal computing and embedded systems. However, the programming environment for multi-core processor based systems is still quite immature and lacks efficient tools. In this work, we present a new VERTAF/Multi-Core framework and show how software code can be automatically generated from SysML models of multi-core embedded systems. We illustrate how model-driven design based on SysML can be seamlessly integrated with Intel's threading building blocks (TBB) and the Quantum Platform middleware libraries. We use a digital video recording system to illustrate the benefits of the framework. Our experiments show how the combination of SysML, QP, and TBB help in making the multi-core embedded system programming model-driven, easy, efficient, and effortless.

INTRODUCTION

Multicore architectures have emerged ubiquitously and rapidly in the area ranging from desktop and laptop computers to the embedded systems. For embedded processors such as ARM's Cortex-A9 MPCore [1], Intel's CoreTM 2 Duo E4300, T7500, T7400, L7500, L7400, U7500, Quad-Core Intel Xeon Processor E5300 series [2], multi-core programming for embedded systems is no longer a luxury, but has become a necessity. We need embedded software engineers to be adept in programming such processors; however, the reality is that very few engineers know how to program them. The current state-of-the-art technology in multicore programming is based on the use of language extensions such as OpenMP [3] or libraries such as Intel Threading Building Block (TBB) [4]. Both OpenMP and TBB are very useful when programmers are already experts in multithreading and multicore programming; however, for the vast majority of programmers and embedded software designers, there still exists a tremendous challenge in this urgent transition from unicore systems to multicore systems. To accelerate the adoption of parallel programming technologies by embedded software designers, we extend our tool, *Verifiable Embedded Real-Time Application Framework* (VERTAF) [5], for multi-core embedded software design and verification. VERTAF is a UML-based application framework for embedded real-time software design and verification, and it is also an integration of software component-based reuse, formal synthesis, and formal verification.

Our primary goal is model-driven architecture (MDA) development for multicore embedded software. Several issues crop up when developing a model-driven architecture for multicore embedded software. First of all, how much and what kinds of explicit parallelism must be specified by a software engineer through system modeling. Second, how can we automatically and correctly realize the user-specified models into multi-core embedded software code. Third, how do we test and validate the generated code. Finally, how do we apply a software engineering process to the development of multi-core embedded software. We will detail the partial solutions to the above issues in this chapter, which are still open to more research work.

The organization of this chapter is as follows. Section 2 gives the preliminaries for the readers to understand the underlying work of VMC. In Section 3, we describe the control flow of VMC framework, and detail design of each component in the framework. Section 4 illustrates the experiment results, including the performance analysis and power consumption. Section 5 describes the conclusions and future works.

---

*Address correspondence to Dr. Pao-Ann Hsiung: Department of Computer Science and Information Engineering, National Chung Cheng University, 168, University Road, Min-Hsiung, Chiayi-62102, Taiwan, ROC; Tel.: +886-5-2720411 ext. 33119; E-mail: pahsiung@cs.ccu.edu.tw

PRELIMINARIES

VERTAF/Multi-Core (VMC) is an extension of VERTAF, which is a UML-based application framework that takes three types of extended UML models [6], namely Class Diagrams with deployments, timed state machines, and extended sequence diagrams. The sequence diagrams are translated into *Power-Aware Real-Time Petri Nets* and then scheduled for low-power design along with satisfaction of memory constraints. The timed state machines are translated into *Extended Timed Automata* (ETA) and model checked using the SGM (*State Graph Manipulators*) model checker. The class diagram and the state machines are used for code generation.

The *Unified Modeling Language* (UML) is an industry de-facto standard language used for designing software from various application domains, including embedded systems. UML allows software designers to visualize, and document models of their software. In order to analyze, design, and verify complex systems, an extension of UML called the OMG System Modeling Language (SysML) [7] was recently proposed. SysML reuses several components from UML and extends the system requirements model by supporting more diagrams, such as requirement and parametric diagrams where the former is used for requirements engineering and the latter is used for performance analysis and quantitative analysis. Thus, in this work, instead of using UML as in VERTAF, we have started to adopt SysML as our modeling language in VMC.

VERTAF uses the *Quantum Platform* (QP) [8] for embedded software code generation because QP provides programmers designing well-structured embedded applications which are a set of concurrency executing hierarchical state machines. QP also helps to rapidly implement software in an object-oriented fashion. A SysML state machine can be implemented by a QP *Active Object*. Based on the programming principles and APIs provided by QP, VERTAF translates a system modeled by a user with UML state machines into C/C++ embedded software code. The generated code based on QP framework is lightweight and easily portable across different embedded software platforms. In VMC, QP is still adopted to implement the state machine of SysML model.

Besides QP, VMC also adopts Intel's *Threading Building Blocks* (TBB) as its foundational library for multi-core software. TBB is a library, expressing parallelism in a C++ program, which helps us to leverage multi-core processor performance without having to be a threading expert. It represents a higher-level, task-based parallelism that abstracts platform details and threading mechanisms for performance and scalability. TBB realizes the concept of scalability in writing efficient scalable programs, *i.e.* a program can benefit from the increasing number of processor cores. Nevertheless, it requires expertise in parallel programming before a software engineer can correctly apply the different parallel programming interfaces provided by TBB. TBB tasks are the basic logical units of computation. The library provides a task scheduler, which is the engine that drives the algorithm templates. The scheduler maps the TBB tasks onto TBB threads. The scheduler tries to trade off between memory demands and cross-thread communication by evaluating the task graph which is a directed graph. The node in the task graph represents task, and the edge from the node points to the task's parent task waiting for its completion or NULL task. The scheduler processes the tasks in a task graph in two ways, including the depth-first and breadth-first executions, which can be seen as sequential execution and concurrent execution, respectively. The breadth-first scheduling consumes more memory than the depth-first scheduling. The scheduler also performs task stealing when a thread's task queue is empty. The task stealing strategy achieves better load balancing among cores.

In order to support code optimization, the multi-core library, OpenMP, is also adapted in the VMC framework. OpenMP (Open Multi-Processing) is an application programming interface (API) that supports multi-platform shared memory multiprocessing programming in C, C++ and FORTRAN on many architectures, including Unix and Microsoft Windows platforms. It consists of a set of compiler directives, library routines, and environment variables that influence run-time behavior. Jointly defined by a group of major computer hardware and software vendors, OpenMP is a portable, scalable model that gives programmers a simple and flexible interface for developing parallel applications for platforms ranging from the desktop to the supercomputer. An application built with the hybrid model of parallel programming can run on a computer cluster using both OpenMP and Message Passing Interface (MPI), or more transparently through the use of OpenMP extensions for non-shared memory systems. If a "for loop" can be parallelized, we can simply add OpenMP directive before the loop.

VERTAF/MULTI-CORE (VMC) FRAMEWORK

VMC is extended from VERTAF to support multicore programming. The system design flow in VMC is illustrated in Fig. **1**. Software synthesis is defined as a two-phase process: a machine-independent software construction phase and a machine-dependent software implementation phase. This separation helps us to plug-in different target languages, middleware, real-time operating systems, and hardware device configurations. We call the two phases as frontend and backend phases.

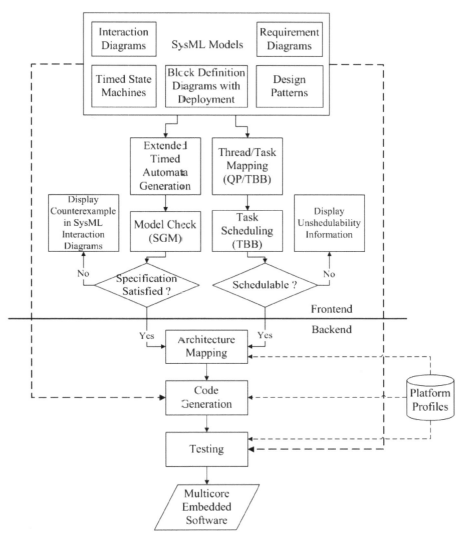

Figure 1: VMC framework design flow.

The frontend phase is further divided into three sub-phases, namely SysML modeling phase, real-time embedded software scheduling phase, and formal verification phase. There are three sub-phases in the back-end phase, namely architecture mapping, code generation, and testing. To achieve the goals of the design flow and integrate each phases in the flow, seven components are used to compose the functionality of the VMC framework. We will use these components to describe each phase, and how the VMC framework can support the multicore programming.

Fig. **2** shows the relationships among the seven components, including Requirements Modeling (RM), Design Modeling (DM), Model Repository (MR), Code Generation (CG), Architecture Mapping (AM), Code Optimization (CO), and Code Testing (CT). The RM and DM components take the responsibility of the SysML modeling in the phase of the frontend in VMC design flow. The components, including AM, CG, CO and CT, are in charge of the phases, namely the architecture mapping, code generation, and testing. The two phases, namely the real-time embedded software scheduling phase, and the formal verification phase, are implicitly implemented by CG component which will be detailed in this chapter later. The component MR provides the multi-view integration model and reusable component database for the other components to exchange data and access required elements for its own processing.

In the following subsection, we will described the detail design of each component in the VMC design flow and illustrate how these components can achieve multi-core programming.

Requirements Modeling (RM)

In the requirements modeling (RM) component, we adopted a model driven requirement modeling process based on SysML, which is based on the IDE tool and SysML modeling tool, Eclipse and Papyrus, respectively.

Fig. **3** shows the system structure of the modeling process. We make use of SysML profile for the requirements template. The diagrams of SysML bear relevant information of the requirements. The system users are defined as relevant personnel of software development such as manager, system analyst of the special project, etc. The purpose lies in helping users to set up intact requirements, and guide, cause users to input the correct requirements documents content, and allow quantization of requirements (Requirement Quantization). The use of quantized unit can help user, when setting up the requirements, in preventing inaccurate requirements description. It can also reduce the equivocal requirements specifications during modeling stage which causes the waste of development cost and time.

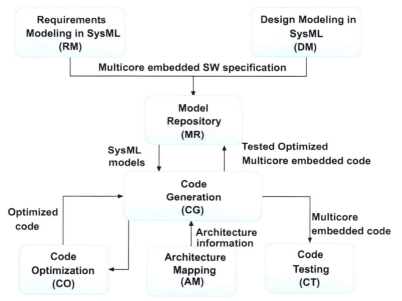

Figure 2: Components of VMC framework architecture.

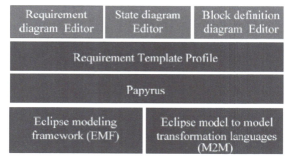

Figure 3: Architecture of modeling process.

The first step in the system development is writing requirements documents. The quality of the requirements documents will influence the progress of the procedure of special project. We hope user, in the course of requirements modeling, can let each requirements model attach intact requirements information. Fig. **4** illustrates the procedures for the requirements information based on the MDA structure. The system analyst draws out SysML requirements diagrams (Fig. **5**) separately for each requirement according to the requirement profile templates content of the requirements in CIM stage. Each requirements classification (Requirement class) owns a corresponding profile template. Functional requirements examples were shown as Table **1**.

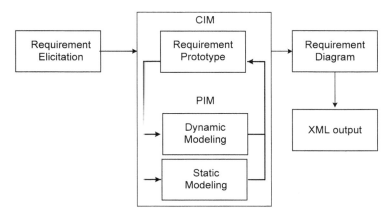

Figure 4: Requirements information setup flow.

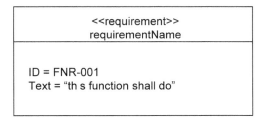

Figure 5: Requirement legend of requirement diagram.

Table 1: An Example of Functional Requirement Template

Profile	Content
Classified Catalogue	Functional
Requirement Name	Connection Server
Requirement ID	VSS-FNR-002
Project Name	VMC_SYN
Creator	Joe
Date	2009.5.1
.....	...

Through analyzing the preliminary requirements question template and preliminary requirements diagram, the initial requirements association is built. Following this, the prototype of SysML requirements diagram is described according to this association relationship. We then cooperate with the use case diagram to facilitate distinguishing system scope and functionalities fast. This not only promotes the overall integrality of the requirements, but also facilitates estimation of the development cost and time.

We explain the operation about the personnel, procedure, system and the rule of its state's transition according to the state diagram analysis at PIM stage. We then define the operation (operation) of the requirements, and the behavioral definition attribute of conversion (Attribute) of the state based on the movements shift within the state diagram between every state. Information received is summarized as in Table **2**. These information will be consulted and used in block definition diagram to express system static structure. The Block Definition Diagram (hereafter referred to as BDD) is defined as in Fig. **6**. Usually BDD is regarded as an important blueprint for designing the system. The analyst constructs the preliminary static structure of system (that is to say the BDD) through applying the requirements profile template mechanically. More attributes and operation information is gathered and learned to join BDD by analyzing the preceding state diagram and the requirements templates. Table **2** defines the operation when the state transition movements.

Table 2: State Transition Operations

System Name	
A. Transition Action B. Transition Behavior	a. Operation Definition b. Attribute Definition

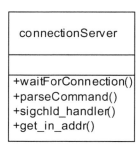

Figure 6: Connection server block definition diagram.

We also make use of OC to standardize user's narration way at the time of inputting Profiles. The requirements contents user inputs can be verified against the OCL field conditions, thus preventing user from inputting improper data or requirements documents content. Table **3** shows one example of employing the OCL on the terms from one of the template.

Table 3: An Example of OCL Condition Constraints

Condition	Data type	Constraint	OCL definition
Client number	Integer	The value must greater than "1"	Self.CleintNum>0

Design Modeling (DM)

A design pattern usually describes the solution context in which it is a well-designed structure, and the judgment of a suitable pattern fully relies on the developer's knowledge and experience with it. Without having rich experience and knowing the applicability with a pattern significantly limits the use of it. To address this issue, we propose an approach for specifying the applicable context and refinement steps of patterns, and automating the refinement process. This approach systematically guides one to specify the problem context and the refinement steps of a pattern in general modeling approaches. Both problem and solution contexts are documented in UML profile, respectively, and the refinement steps between them are described in formal transformation rules. DM automates the design refinement by model transformation, which aids developers identifying operations which could be parallel processing, and revising a sequential design as a parallel structure.

As presented in Fig. **7**, we keep the pattern description which follows GoF style [9] with different sections, such as motivation, consequence, etc. in addition to the specifications of I_F(functional requirement intent), I_N(non-functional requirement intent), S_F(functional requirement structure), S_N(non-functional requirement structure), T. The pattern repository provides a knowledge base to store valuable and reusable pattern information. Through pattern modeling approach, sophisticated developers can define the functional content (I_F, S_F) and non-functional content (I_N, S_N) of a pattern for various design purposes or requirements. The pattern transformation provides developers to specify the evolution process from S_F to S_N in formal transformation language by rule editor, or revise a raw design to an enhanced one through transformation engine based on the transformation specification. When system developers select a pattern to apply, the transformation specification is loaded in the transformation engine automatically.

Our approach revises a raw design to an enhanced design through the model transformation based on the evolution process for applying a pattern, thus we call it *pattern-based model transformation*. The transformation represents the essence of a design pattern. The mode transformation MT maps a S_F design to a S_N design. That is, $\forall s \in S_F(dp), MT(s) \in S_N(dp)$, where the notation $\in$ denotes the *instantiation* relationship between model and metamodel. $s \in S$ means that the model s is an instance model of the metamodel S. Fig. **8** depicts this concept of pattern-based model transformation. First, we have to design $S_F(dp)$ and $S_N(dp)$ of a design pattern dp at the metamodel level respectively. Roles in a pattern profile are played by model elements in a design at model level. We describe pattern roles by stereotypes with tagged-values and constraints which are UML profile extension mechanisms to avoid inventing new notations for new concepts.

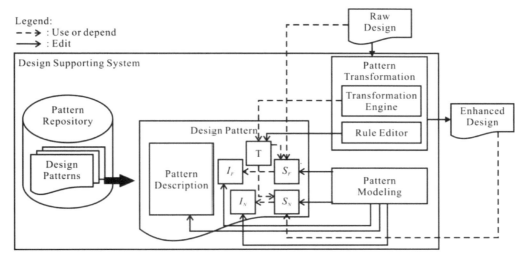

Figure 7: The overall architecture of DM.

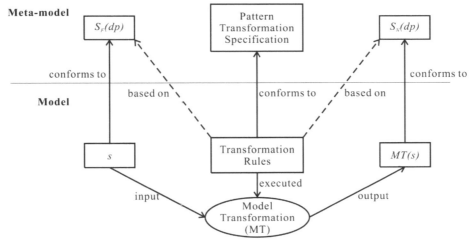

Figure 8: The concept of pattern-based model transformation.

In the meanwhile, we have to design the transformation specification which describes the mapping rules from $S_F(dp)$ to $S_N(dp)$ formally. These mapping rules specify which roles are added or removed from $S_F(dp)$ to $S_N(dp)$ during the evolution process, such as add a new abstract class, add a new operation into a class or remove an association between one and the other class, etc. So far, we have a raw design s which is an instance of $S_F(dp)$. After describing the transformation specification, we can transform s to an enhanced design $MT(s)$ by executing mapping function $MT()$ based on the transformation specification. Finally, we can get the well-designed model conforming to $S_N(dp)$ automatically.

As a whole, system designers can pick up a pattern which is appropriate for improving a raw design from pattern repository, and the raw design conforms to the S_F of the pattern. Based on rules of the pattern's transformation specification, a pattern is applied to the raw design which is converted to an enhanced design automatically.

Code Generation (CG) and Architecture Mapping (AM)

The CG component receives system models from the RM and DM components. The CG component chooses four diagrams for a user to input as system specification models, namely requirement diagram, extended interaction diagram, block definition diagram, and timed state machine. The four diagrams are restricted, as well as, enhanced for modeling multi-core embedded software.

Requirement Diagram

For multi-core embedded systems, a designer can specify the functional or non-functional requirements of his/her system such as the encoding or streaming rates in terms of the number of video frames per second for a multimedia system.

Extended Interaction Diagram

Interaction diagrams are mapped to formal Petri net models for scheduling.

Block Definition Diagram with Hardware Deployment

On a block definition diagram a deployment relation is used for specifying the deployment of a software object on a hardware object.

Timed State Machine

State machines are extended with real-time clocks that can be reset and values checked for state transition triggering.

Parallel design patterns can be modeled by the four SysML models. In the DM component, some predefined parallel design patterns such as parallel pipeline, parallel tasks, and parallel loops are provided such that system designers can use them to model parallelism in his/her system.

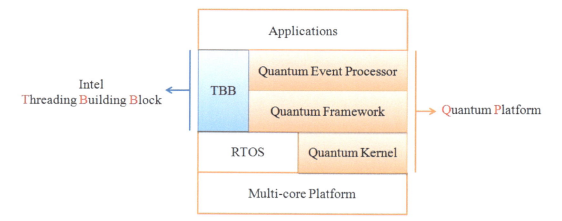

Figure 9: Code architecture.

For the Thread/Task Mapping and Scheduling, Each state machine is mapped to an active object in QP. Design patterns for multi-core programming are mapped to parallel tasks and task graphs in the TBB terminology. The QP active objects and TBB tasks are all executed by user-level pthreads, which are then mapped one-to-one to the Linux OS kernel threads. The threads associated to QP active objects are scheduled by the POSIX library, and the TBB threads are scheduled by the TBB library along with thread migration among different cores for load balancing. Fig. **9** shows the code architecture in the CG component. We adopt a multi-tier approach for code generation: an application layer, a middleware layer (Quantum Platform), a multi-core threading library layer (TBB), an operating system layer, and a multi-core platform layer. Since both QP and TBB are very small in size and very efficient in performance, they are quite suitable for real-time embedded system software implementation. In the operating system layer, we adopt Linux as our target operating system. VMC currently supports PB11MPCore and Intel's processor architecture running the Linux OS.

For verification phase in frontend of VMC design flow, We modeled real-time task scheduling, task migration between processor cores, and several load balancing policies into the SGM model checker, which is used in VMC to formally verify the automata models by combining simulation and model checking techniques to evaluate the system performance. We can initialize and configure the software and hardware by the evaluation results. The methodology is proposed in [10].

The AM component defines several hardware classes specified in the deployments of the SysML block definition diagram, which are supported by VMC through platform profiles. The architecture mapping phase then becomes simply the configuration of the hardware system and operating system through the automatic generation of configuration files, make files, header files, and dependency files. Multi-core processor architecture configurations can also be set in this phase. For example, the number of processor cores available, the number of cores to be used, the number of TBB threads, the amount of buffer space, the number of network connections, the amount of hard disk space available, the number and type of I/O devices available, the security mechanisms, and the allowed level of processor core loadings are some of the configurations to be set in this phase. VMC currently supports PB11MPCore [11], which is a platform baseboard with a quad ARM11MPCore multi-core processor running the Linux OS.

Code Optimization (CO)

The main goal of this component is to state the design and implementation of parallel program optimization supporting for VMC embedded software on Multicore architecture. At first, we make use of compiler technologies, such as the data dependency analysis and software pipelining for implementing parallel instruction, parallel loop partitioning, and loop scheduling and optimization. OpenMP is suitable for the work as described in Section 2. With supporting directives OpenMP helps to extend the limitations of the Fortran and C/C++ language and supports not only long, regular loop, but also irregular constructs such as while loops and recursive structures.

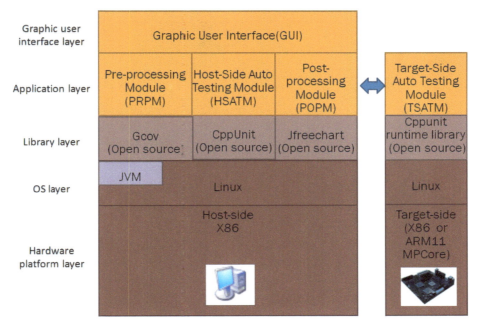

Figure 10: Code testing architecture.

Code Testing (CT)

We proposed the Automatic Testing Environment for Multi-core Embedded Software (ATEMES) system for the CT component as shown in Fig. **10**. The testing environment of ATEMES system can be seen as a 5-layer architecture. The bottom layer is hardware platform layer. On host-side, we have used X86 Platforms. Platforms of target-side can be X86 or ARM11 MPCore. The 2nd layer is OS layer. On both sides, we have used Linux operation system. The 3rd layer is the library layer adopting the open sources, including GCOV [12], Cppunit [13], and Jfreechart [14]. The 4th layer is application layer constructed by ATEMES system modules. The 5th layer is the graphic user interface layer of host-side.

The architecture of ATEMES is composed of four parts: Pre-Processing Module (PRPM), Host-Side Auto-Testing Module (HSATM), Target-Side Auto-Testing Module (TSATM), and Post-Processing Module (POPM). Testing functions provided by ATEMES system include coverage testing, unit testing, performance testing and race condition testing. In VMC, we focus on coverage testing and unit testing. Fig. **11** illustrates the architecture of ATEMES modules. Functions of respective modules are detailed as follows. Fig. **12** shows the example of teset case framework automatically generated, and shows the example of test driver automatically generated.

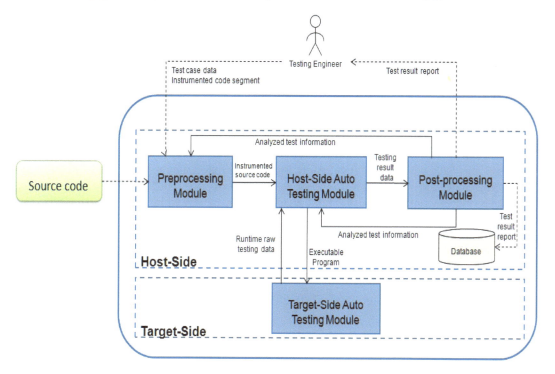

Figure 11: ATEMES system architecture.

```
void TestDriver::test_structTest()
{
    int index=testCaseParser.getIndex("structTest");
    Data a;
    a.name = testCaseParser.testCase[index][0];
    a.age = atoi(testCaseParser.testCase[index+1]);
    a.address = atof(testCaseParser.testCase[index+2]);
    int b =atoi(testCaseParser.testCase[index+3]);
    int c =atoi(testCaseParser.testCase[index+4]);
    int result =atoi(testCaseParser.testCase[index+5]);
    CPPUNIT_ASSERT( result == TESTEDFILE.structTest(a,b,c) );
    }
}
```

Figure 12: Test case framework example.

```
CPPUNIT_NS::OStringStream stream;
 TestCaseParser testCaseParser;
testCaseParser.parserTestCase();

CPPUNIT_NS::TestResult controller;

CPPUNIT_NS::TestResultCollector result;
controller.addListener( &result );

CPPUNIT_NS::BriefTestProgressListener progress;
controller.addListener( &progress );

CPPUNIT_NS::TestRunner runner;
runner.addTest( CPPUNIT_NS::TestFactoryRegistry::getRegistry().makeTest() );
runner.run( controller );

CPPUNIT_NS::CompilerOutputter outputter1( &result, CPPUNIT_NS::stdCOut() );
outputter1.write();
//Write file to Result.xml.
CPPUNIT_NS::XmlOutputter outputter2( &result, stream );
outputter2.write();
std::string actualXml = stream.str();
ofstream fout("Result.xml");
fout<<actualXml;
fout.close();
```

Figure 13: Test driver example.

Pre-Processing Testing Module

PRPM module is in control of the pre-processing testing tasks, including parsing source code, automatically generating test case and test input data, and automatically instrument source code so that data can be collected during the execution of target program and report to host-side during runtime.

Host-Side and Target-Side Automatic Testing Module

Tasks of automatic testing are completed by two modules, which are the HSATM module on the host-side, and the TSATM module on the target-side. The main function of HSATM module is to automatically generating test driver based on cppunit library, and automatically compiling test driver and instrumented source code to executable files. The executable files and test input data are then delivered to target-side for execution. The major task of TSATM module is to trigger test driver to execute or terminate testing tasks, and can monitor profiler to collect testing data. It can return collected testing information to host-side during runtime.

Testing Post-Processing Module

POPM module takes charge of the post-processing testing tasks, mainly by parsing the collected data as reference for the next round of automatically generated testing data. To make it easy to get across the test result, outcome of the test result is presented in visualized way. Graphical interface is adopted to present test result during runtime or the end of testing. The modules are composed of 2 parts, test log analyzer and test result presentation module.

We now discuss the testing scenario, called Multi-Round Testing Scenario, for the ATEMES System as shown in Fig. **14**. Multi-round automatic testing scenario is selected to describe how the system operates. The scenario of multi-round automatic testing is parsing source code, generating the intended data including test case, test input data, instrument code segment and test driver, automatically executing testing, collecting and parsing test log file, automatically executing the next round testing task based on the parsed outcome until testing termination conditions are met. Actions are as follows:

Step 1. PRPM read source code.

Step 2. With the aid of information provided by requirement specification files, PRPM conducts parsing source code which has been read and extracts program function name and parameter, internal structure of program, and other information.

Step 3. PRPM analyzes the extracted information based on the parsed data by step 2. Test case is generated automatically after analysis, or new test case (test input data) is generated based on the test result feedback by POPM during testing.

Step 4. PRPM processes the extracted information based on the parsed data by step 3. Analysis is conducted according to the intended testing items. Instrumented source code is automatically generated after analysis.

Step 5. HSATM reads test case data generated from PRPM.

Step 6. HSATM automatically generates test drivers based on the data collected by PRPM.

Step 7. HSATM reads the instrumented source code generated from PRPM.

Step 8. HSATM compiles the instrumented source code and test driver to target-side executable files and uploads to TSATM.

Step 9. TSATM is triggered to execute automatic testing. It collects the test result logs and returns to HSATM.

Step 10. HSATM recives the test result logs executed by TSATM and passes to POPM module to analysis and statistics.

Step 11. Repeat step 3 to step 10 until testing termination conditions are met.

Step 12. POPM presents test result to testing engineer.

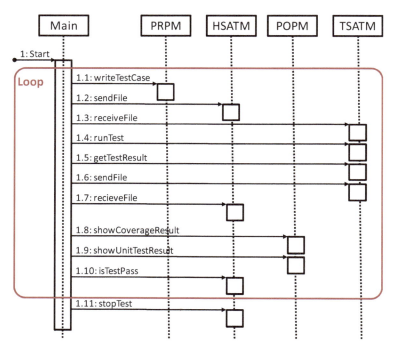

Figure 14: The sequence diagram of multi-round testing.

Model Repository (MR)

The main goal of the last component in VMC framework is as follows.

    i.   To design a Unified Model for supporting the whole VMC project software life cycle.

ii.   Issues the constrain, practice, confliction and analysis in devising the multi-core embedded system software design in practical way.

iii.   To design and develop editor that support Repository and Unify Model Schema.

iv.   Multi-view supported model and integration for the various stages.

In our approach, we use an XML-based unified meta-model (XUMM) to define the schema of an XML-based unified model (XUM). This allows us to consolidate and coordinate modeling information from the adopted paradigms — such as analysis and design models represented in SysML, design patterns, framework, etc. — in each phase of the software life cycle.

As shown in Fig. **15**, based on XUMM, sub-models are unified, integrated, and represented as views of an XUM. Semantics in each sub-model should be described explicitly and transferred precisely in XUM.

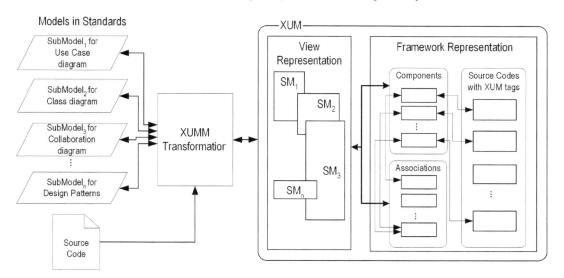

Figure 15: The unification and integration of models into XUM.

Fig. **16** shows the relationship of views in XUM. The major merits of XUM are (1) the modeling information used in models (views) of each phase of the software life cycle and (2) the interaction and relationship of models (views). Both are explicitly defined and represented in XUM.

The relationship of the XUMM with an XUM is similar to that of a DTD with an XML document. XUMM defines the schema (definitions) of an XUM. Three kinds of elements defined in XUMM describe the constitution of an XUM; they are component, association, and unification relation. Any object in an XUM is identified as a component. Components and associations describe the semantic information of model objects and their relationships, respectively. The third kind of element, unification relation, describes the relationship of different views.

Software maintenance constitutes a major part of the total cost occurring during the life span of a software system, our approach will helps software engineers to understand relations and dependencies among different model and improve maintainability.

EXPERIMENT RESULTS

Due to the limitation of porting TBB to ARM11 MPCore, we currently implemented DVR system on Intel Core2 Quad CPU, Q6600 2.4 GHz, with 2GB RAM. Several metric are measured in this experiment, including the performance, power consumption, and the load balancing. Two different versions of the implementations are compared, which one version is implementation by QP only, called the QP version, and the other version is implemented by TBB and QP, called the TBB version. Several parameters are also used to configure our experiment, which are the number of cores, number of connections for real-time video streaming, the number of digital cameras and the capture rate of raw videos.

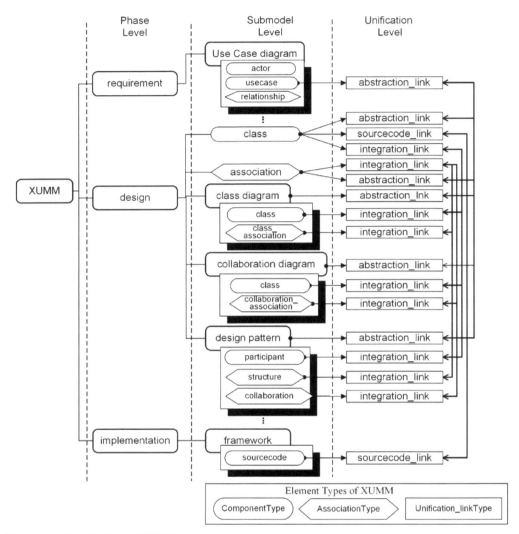

Figure 16: The relationship of views in XUM.

In the first experiment, we observed at the load balance of processor cores. We compared the QP and TBB version with the configuration of 4 cores, 1 real-time streaming, 2 cameras and 16 20 fps capture rate. As shown in Fig. **17**, the TBB does provide the load balancing between cores.

In the second experiment, we measured the performance by the encoding rate in frame per second (fps). The configuration of this experiment is the same as in the first experiment. As illustrated in Fig. **18**, the average encoding rate of QP version is 12 fps while the average encoding rate in TBB version is about 16 fps. We can see that the TBB pipeline did provide the better performance than the QP version due to the TBB concurrently processes more than one blocks of a raw frame. TBB pipeline reduces the time when encoding each raw image frame.

We then configured the second experiment into different parameters which the number of cores is reduced to three and two cores. We limited both the QP and TBB threads to use only two or three cores through the linux system call, that is sched_setaffinity. With three cores, the average encoding rate of QP version still kept in 12 fps, but the TBB version dropped to 6.13 fps. With two cores, the encoding rate of QP version dropped to 9.78 fps, and the TBB version is 6.58 fps. We can observe that the less the cores can be used, the worse is the performance provided by

TBB. That is because the TBB introduces the overhead of splitting and merging parallel tasks. The phenomenon is more obviously when the number of cores is reduced. As to the streaming rate in the first and second experiments, the streaming rate is consistency with the encoding rate which we connected for real-time streaming. That is because the streaming tasks are I/O bound.

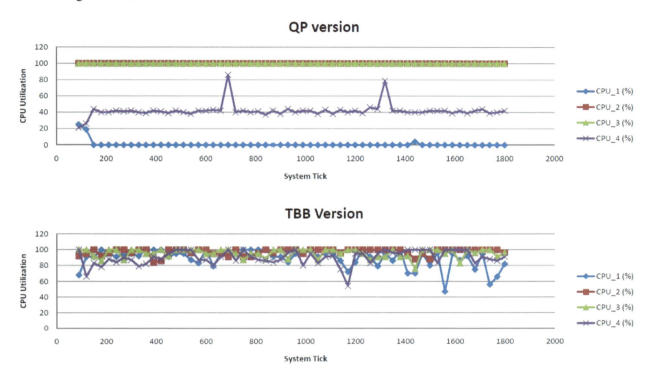

Figure 17: Comparison of load balance.

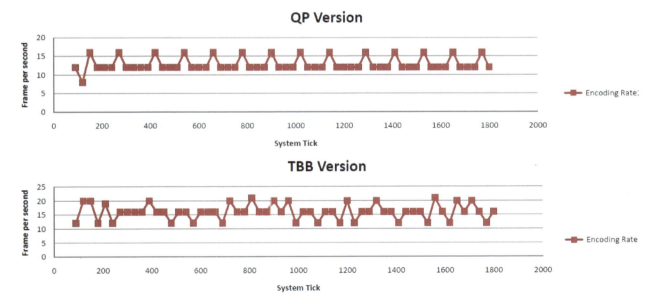

Figure 18: Performance of encoding rate.

The third experiment shows the power consumption of the QP and TBB versions. We evaluated the power consumption according to the core utilization. We adopted the power model proposed by Lien *et al.* [15], and represented by the following equation

$$P = D + (M - D) * \alpha U^{\beta}$$

where P represents the average power consumption in Watts, and D represents base power in Watts when CPU is idle, and M represents the full-load power consumption in Watts, and U is for the CPU utilization, and finally, α and β are the parameters which are set to be 1 and 0.5 respectively. We also set D to 69 Watts and M to 142, according to the hardware configuration of the target platform. The configuration of this experiment is the same to the first one with 4 core, 1 real-time streaming, 2 cameras, and 16-20 fps capture rate.

As shown in Fig. **19**, the TBB Version consumes more power during 1800 system ticks which the total energy is 8076.291 Watts compared to the QP Version in 7274.522 Watts. TBB keeps all CPU core in busy while doing the load-balance, such that it also consumes more energy, but also increase the performance in first experiment.

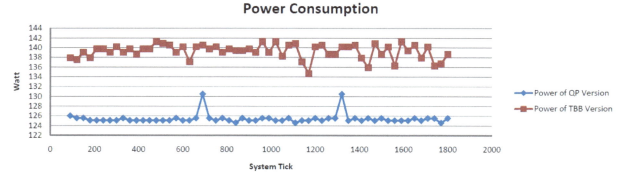

Figure 19: Power consumption.

CONCLUSIONS AND FUTURE WORK

VERTAF/Multi-Core (VMC) is an application framework for developing multi-core embedded software. It adopts a model-driven approach with automatic code generation from SysML models. The code generated by VMC uses the Quantum Platform (QP) APIs and the Intel's Threading Building Blocks (TBB) library along with an operating system that supports multi-core processors such as Linux. VMC shows how easy it is to develop embedded software for multi-core processors. We used a real-world example, namely a digital video recording (DVR) system, to illustrate how VMC solves several of the issues related to model-driven development for multi-core embedded systems.

VMC currently supports homogenous multi-core platform. In the future work, we will try to extend VMC to support heterogeneous multi-core platforms consisting of general-purpose multi-core processors and digital signal processors.

REFERENCES

[1]   ARM Cortex-A9 MPCore. Retrieved July 7, 2010, from http://www.arm.com/products/CPUs/ARMCortex-A9_MPCore.html.

[2]   Intel   Quad-Core   Xeon   Processor   5300   Series.   Retrieved   July   7,   2010,   from
        http://www.intel.com/design/intarch/quadcorexeon/5300/index.htm.

[3]   OpenMP. Retrieved July 7, 2010, from http://www.openmp.org.

[4]   Reinders J. Intel Threading Building Blocks: Outfitting C++ for Multi-core Processor Parallelism. O'Reilly Media, Inc., 2007.

[5]   Hsiung P.A., Lin S.W., Tseng C.H., *et al.* VERTAF: An application framework for the design and verification of embedded
        real-time software. IEEE Transac Software Engin, October 2004; 30(10): 656–674.

[6]   Rumbaugh J, Booch G, & Jacobson I. The UML Reference Guide. Addison Wesley Longman. 1999.

[7]   SysML. Retrieved July 7, 2010, from http://www.sysml.org/.

[8]   QP, What is QP™. Quantum Leaps®, LLC. Retrieved July 7, 2010, from http://www.state-machine.com/products/.

[9]   Gamma E, Helm R, Johnson R, and Vlissides J. Design patterns: elements of reusable software. Addison-Wesley 1994.

[10]   Tsao, CC. An Efficient Collaborative Verification Methodology for Multiprocessor SoC with Run-Time Task Migration. Master Thesis. Department of Computer Science and Information Engineering, National Chung Cheng University, Taiwan 2008.

[11]   ARM The Architecture for the Digital World. Hardware Platforms. Retrieved July 7, 2010, from http://www.arm.com/products/DevTools/PB11MPCore.html.

[12]   GCC. the GNU Compiler Collection. Retrieved July 7, 2010, from http://gcc.gnu.org/.

[13]   CppUnit. What is CppUnit?. Retrieved July 7, 2010, from http://sourceforge.net/apps/mediawiki/cppunit/index.php?title=Main_Page.

[14]   JFreeChart. Welcome To JFreeChart. Retrieved July 7, 2010, from http://www.jfree.org/jfreechart/.

[15]   Lien CH, Bai YW, and Lin MB. Estimation by software for the power consumption of streaming-media servers. IEEE Transac Instrument Measur 2007; 56(5): 1859–1870.

CHAPTER 5

Automatic High-Level Code Generation for Multi-Core Processors in Embedded Systems

Yu-Shin Lin, Shang-Wei Lin, Chao-Sheng Lin, Chun-Hsien Lu, Chia-Chiao Ho, Yi-Luen Chang, Bo-Hsuan Wang, and Pao-Ann Hsiung*

Department of Computer Science and Information Engineering, National Chung Cheng University, Chiayi-62102, Taiwan, ROC.

Abstract: This chapter demonstrates how high-level code is automatically generated for multi-core processors. The code generation capability of the *Verifiable Embedded Real-Time Application Framework* (VERTAF) was extended to support multi-core processors in the new VERTAF/Multi-Core (VMC) framework for embedded systems. After users specify embedded software requirements *via* SysML models along with parallel task, parallel data, and parallel dataflow specifications, the code generator automatically generates parallel code. Using the *digital video recording* (DVR) system as a case study, we show the correctness and advantages of the VMC code generator. The main inputs of VMC code generator include the block definition diagrams, state machine diagrams, and requirement diagrams of the system to be designed. The proposed code generation in VMC not only significantly decreases the amount of manually-written code, but also provides a formal procedure for model-conforming code generation of multi-core embedded software.

INTRODUCTION

Multi-core processors are becoming prevalent in personal computing and have proliferated embedded processor designs. Nevertheless, the current state-of-the-art of multi-core processor programming is based on the use of language extensions or libraries, such as *OpenMP* [6], Intel's *Threading Building Blocks* (TBB) [6], [9], and Microsoft's *Task Parallel Library* (TPL) [14] that require parallel computing expertise and experience. Also, the programming environment for multi-core processors is still quite immature and lacks efficient development tools. To accelerate the adoption of parallel programming technologies for embedded software designers, we extended our previous work, *Verifiable Embedded Real-Time Application Framework* (VERTAF) [1], and proposed a new framework called *VERTAF/Multi-Core* (VMC) [3-5] to show how parallel code for embedded systems can be automatically generated from high-level *System Modeling Language* (SysML) [11] models, which is a profile of *Unified Modeling Language* (UML) [15].

VERTAF is a UML-based application framework for embedded real-time software design and verification. It is mainly an integration of software component-based reuse, formal synthesis, and formal verification. It takes as input three types of extended UML models, namely class diagrams with deployments, timed statecharts, and extended sequence diagrams. The sequence diagrams are translated into *Power-Aware Real-Time Petri Nets* and then scheduled for low-power design along with satisfaction of memory constraints. The timed statecharts are translated into *Extended Timed Automata* (ETA) and model checked using the *State Graph Manipulators* (SGM) model checker [11]. The class diagrams and the statecharts are used for code generation. VERTAF has been successfully applied to various application domains.

VMC is an extension of VERTAF mainly to support multi-core processors in embedded systems. To alleviate the burden of application designers, VMC adopts *model-driven architecture* (MDA) and supports parallel design patterns. A multi-core embedded system application is specified by a set of SysML models, from which code can be automatically generated. The parallel design patterns in VMC include (a) parallel pipeline to hide latency, (b) parallel loop to reduce latency, and (c) parallel tasks to increase throughput. These design patterns correspond precisely to the three real-world concurrency issues, including reducing latency, hiding latency, and increasing throughput [1]. More details on the full VMC framework can be found in Chapter 4 of this book. Here, in this chapter, instead we adopt a case study approach to introduce how VMC actually generates parallel code.

*****Address correspondence to Dr. Pao-Ann Hsiung:** Department of Computer 168, University Road, Min-Hsiung, Chiayi-62102, Taiwan, ROC; Tel.: +886-5-2720411 ext. 33119; E-mail: pahsiung@cs.ccu.edu.tw

This chapter is organized as follows. Section 2 introduces the case study to validate the proposed VMC code generator. Section 3 describes the design flow of VMC and the functionalities of every component of VMC code generator. Section 4 gives a simple conclusion and some future work for code generation.

CASE STUDY

To illustrate and evaluate the VMC code generator, we present a case study of a *digital video recording* (DVR) system, which is a real-time multimedia system used typically in concurrent remote monitoring of multiple sites. The server in a DVR system can perform both real-time and on-demand streaming of videos to multiple clients at the same time. Several digital cameras provide the input images for real-time video streaming, and videos previously recorded are stored for on-demand streaming. DVR system is a good illustration example since it exemplifies all three kinds of parallelism, namely task parallelism, data parallelism, and data flow parallelism.

The architecture of DVR system is illustrated in Fig. **1**, which has three subsystems, namely *Parallel Video Encoder* (PVE), *Video Streaming Server* (VSS), and *Remote Monitor Clients* (RMC). PVE collects videos captured by digital cameras and outputs compressed data after encoding these video frames. VSS has a *database server* to store and manage encoded frames in large video databases. The *encoded data buffer manager* (EDBM) is responsible for temporarily storing encoded video frames before they are stored into secondary storages or before they are transmitted for real-time viewing. The *video streaming manager* (VSM) is responsible for processing requests for video viewing. There is a *connection server* (CS) that helps control and grant video requests. With the help of CS, VSS allows connections from *Remote Monitor Clients* (RMCs), and serves RMCs with real-time video streams and on-demand video streams. RMC offers a user interface for users, *via* which users can watch real-time or on-demand videos by connecting to VSS *via* the Internet.

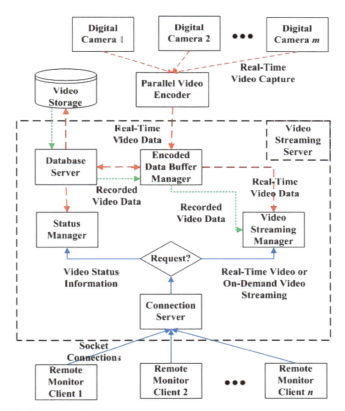

Figure 1: Architecture of digital video recording system.

Taking the architecture of the DVR system as an example, we illustrate how high-level C++ code is generated by VMC from the user-specified SysML models. We will be focusing on the PVE subsystem which is modeled using

SysML block definition diagram, state machine, and requirements diagram. The model for PVE also contains data parallelism constructs, which will be mapped to parallel code by the VMC code generator.

VMC CODE GENERATOR

Before going into the details of the architecture of the VMC code generator and the design flow based on the code generator for a multi-core embedded system development platform, we need to first describe the libraries used as foundations for code generation and the basic architecture of the generated code.

Code Architecture

The architecture of the code generated automatically by VMC is illustrated in Fig. **2**, which uses two libraries as middleware, namely *Quantum Platform* (QP) [11], [16] and *Intel Threading Building Blocks* (TBB) [6], [10]. QP is used as a state machine library that implements the behavior specified by a designer through the state machine models of an application. TBB is used for realizing the parallelism specified in the application model. In the following, we will first describe QP and TBB.

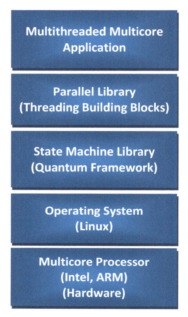

Figure 2: Architecture of code generated by VMC.

Quantum Platform

QP [11], [16] is a C++ library designed specifically for realizing UML state machine models. QP provides a set of application programming interfaces (API) for programmers to implement state machines in software. Both concurrency and hierarchy in the state machines are well supported by QP. Since QP has a very small memory footprint, it has been used in embedded software implementation.

VERTAF was the first framework that supported the automatic code generation based on QP APIs. An application modeled by a set of concurrent hierarchical UML state machines could be automatically implemented by VERTAF using QP. However, VERTAF supported only the old QP version 2.0. VMC now supports the new QP version 4.1.04. Since SysML is a UML profile, QP can also be used to realize SysML state machines, that is, the input models of VMC.

VMC code generator follows the QP mapping semantics between a state machine and an active object, which is QP terminology. Run-to-completion (RTC) semantics is required by UML state machines and thus is also required by the QP APIs. However, this issue is dominant in embedded systems because of the famous never-ending infinite loops in embedded software design. VERTAF proposed a workaround, which is basically implementing an independent state machine that will start running the infinite loop on receiving an initial event. No other events are then required to be processed by this state machine, thus the violation of RTC semantics does not pose any problem. Interactions between this state machine and other state machines can be achieved by other OS-level signaling primitives such as semaphores or events. Note that each active object that implements a state machine is in fact executed by a user-level thread such as POSIX pthread, which in turn is then bound to a kernel-level thread. Thus, communication among active objects using other OS signaling primitives is feasible and fits perfectly with the active objects semantics.

A major advantage in using QP is that the generated code is lightweight and easily portable across different embedded system platforms. As a result, after compiling, the code generated by VMC could be directly executed on different platforms such as a PC with Intel's quad core processor and an embedded system development platform with ARM 11 MPCore processor. The execution results were compared and found to be functionally equivalent, except for the disparity in timing performance and memory usage.

Intel Threading Building Blocks

TBB is Intel's version of how parallelism can be implemented in software that is running on a multi-core processor. Similar to QP, TBB is also a C++ library with a set of APIs that realize well-known parallelism constructs. The three real-world concurrency issues can all be handled using the solutions provided by TBB. Further, TBB helps programmers to leverage multi-core processor performance even if they are not threading experts. The high-level, task-based parallelism realized by TBB is independent of platform details and threading mechanisms, thus high performance and scalability are achieved.

Unlike OpenMP, TBB requires some programming skills and some background knowledge in parallel programming. Nevertheless, VMC opted for using TBB because VMC is a framework for embedded software designers. Currently, we do not expect automatic specification and identification of parallelism in the embedded software domain. Thus, VMC leaves the identification of where parallelism is required to the designers. As long as parallelism is identified correctly by a designer, VMC can automatically transform that abstract model-level specification into actual parallel code based on the TBB APIs.

Since VMC adopts TBB as its parallelism middleware, whatever comes with TBB is naturally packaged into VMC, which in turn, affects the performance of the code generated by VMC. For example, TBB maintains a pool of threads (called *TBB threads*), jobs are specified as *tasks*, tasks are assigned to threads by the TBB scheduler by traversing a task graph using both depth-first and breadth-first, allows random stealing of tasks (task migration) among TBB threads for load balancing, and TBB threads are scheduled by the operating system on the available processor cores.

Though the above-described task-based computation paradigm of TBB is used for realizing parallelism in VMC, yet VMC also performs several customizations, mainly for befitting the embedded system characteristics and requirements. A partial list of customizations in VMC is as follows:

- *Core-specific scheduling*: TBB leaves the actual CPU scheduling of all TBB threads to the underlying operating system such as Linux. To meet embedded and real-time system requirements, VMC allows user-specified *scheduling affinity*, that is, a thread can be scheduled to a specific core. This is achieved in VMC by OS system calls such as `set_sched_affinity()`, `get_sched_affinity()`, etc.

- *Core-utilization management*: TBB tries to leverage the full computation power of all available cores in a processor for high performance execution. However, in an embedded system, there could be multiple objectives, in which performance is only one. Another major objective in an embedded system is low power consumption, which conflicts with the requirement of high performance, in general. As a result, VMC allows specific management of core utilizations because core utilizations directly affect power consumption. In VMC, the model relating power consumption with core utilization in a multi-core processor is adopted from [7]. Given an upper bound on the utilization of a specific core, VMC allows to control scheduling threads on that core once the limit is reached.

- *Extension to heterogeneous multi-core processors*: TBB is designed for homogeneous multi-core processors. The basic assumption in TBB is that all cores have the same computation power and all tasks can be assigned to any thread running on any core. This homogeneity is often violated in a real-world system which contains both multimedia co-processor cores, digital signal processing (DSP) cores, networking cores, graphic processing unit (GPU) cores, and general-purpose processing (GPP) cores. This part of the customization is still an undergoing work. Currently, in VMC, a TBB thread running on a GPP core can act as a host thread that invokes a DSP thread running on a DSP core to process some signal or media data. More work in this direction is urgently required.

Code Generator Architecture

The program synthesis flow of the VMC code generator is illustrated in Fig. **3**, which shows that it is composed of the following five components: model parser, model compiler, parallelism implementer, tree translator, and code emulator. Fig. **4** illustrates the relationships among all the five components, each of which is described as follows.

The model parser is responsible for extracting all related information from user-specified SysML design models, namely block definition diagrams and state machine diagrams. The standard XML schema for UML diagrams is used for parsing the information from these models. An XML semantics tree is generated by the parser, which contains the extracted information from the models and which will also be used as a container for the intermediate code generated in the process of code generation.

The model compiler is in charge of constructing the backbone of the program code, that is, the state machine behavior of each system component. It maps the nodes of the semantics tree to QP code based on the basic mapping primitives found in the QP information files. For example, each state in a state machine diagram is mapped to a static `QState` class, where the `QState` class is defined by QP. Each piece of code is attached to its corresponding node in the semantics tree. This tree with QP code annotation is called a *QP-annotated tree*.

The parallelism implementer is responsible for generating parallel multi-core code, thus parallelization is achieved by this part of the code generator. Each kind of parallelism specification, namely task, data, or data-flow (pipeline), is represented in the SysML models as a UML stereotype and each such stereotype is then associated with a user-customized parallel model. The parallel model is customized from templates provided by VMC. Since VMC uses the TBB library for generating parallel code, a parallel model template is, in fact, a model representation of whatever is supported by TBB. For example, a parallel pipeline from TBB is modeled by a VMC parallel model for pipelines (aka SysML block definition diagram). Searching the QP-annotated tree, if a stereotype is encountered, its corresponding parallel model is referenced and TBB code generated. Note that VMC needs a TBB information file that contains the basic mapping primitives from model-level stereotypes and parallel model to TBB code APIs. Similar to QP code, each piece of TBB code is attached to the corresponding node of the semantics tree. The resulting tree is called a *TBB-annotated tree*.

The components of VMC code generator described until now do not actually generate any program source file into the working directory of a VMC project, because the pieces of code are all annotated to the XML semantics tree. The purpose of proposing and adopting such a code annotation approach is three-folds, as described in the following. First, it allows maximum flexibility between the state machine code (*i.e.* the QP code here) and the parallel code (*i.e.* the TBB code here). Second, the code annotation approach allows VMC to support different versions of the generated code. For example, we can generate QP only code (with limited parallelism and only OS-level load balancing), or code with QP and TBB API invocations (with scalable parallelism and multi-level load balancing). Third, code annotations enable the state machine and the parallel libraries in VMC to be replaced with other user-preferred libraries, without affecting the way in which code is generated. For example, TPL could be used instead of TBB in the VMC framework; however, TPL information files will be required to be integrated into VMC.

Whenever the program source files are to be generated for a particular version of the system program, a corresponding annotated tree is parsed by the tree translator and the corresponding code constructed from the code annotations on each node of the tree. The source code files can be distinguished into two types, namely header files or program files. The SysML block definition diagrams are used to generate a part of the header file, consisting of the active object definitions, without the state declarations. The state information can be found only in the state machine diagrams. The state machines are mainly used to generate the program source files, consisting of the definitions of all states, including the state transition information.

Finally, the code emulator executes the generated code on the target platform to test its functional and non-functional properties. A monitor was implemented in VMC especially for the code emulator to check the core utilizations and user-specified non-functional properties at runtime. For example, the network streaming rate or the multimedia encoding rate could be monitored by VMC and provided as feedback to the code emulator. Suggestions for code optimization *via* detection of performance bottlenecks can be accomplished through the code emulator. This part of the VMC framework is still under-development. The evolution and iterative refinements of the multi-core software code will be a major focus of this code emulator in the future.

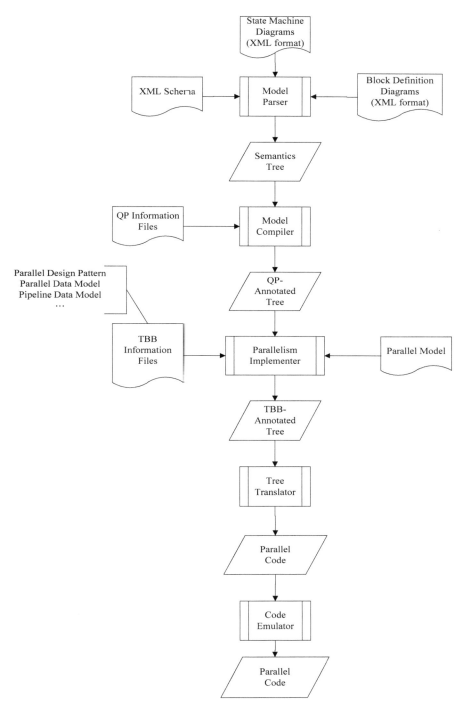

Figure 3: Design flow in the VMC code generator.

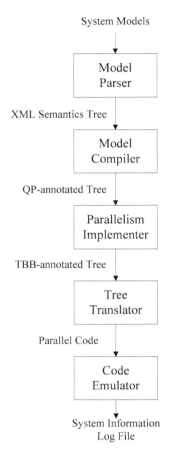

Figure 4: Relationships among components of the VMC code generator.

DVR PVE Case Study

In the rest of this section, we will introduce how VMC implements each of the five components of the code generator. We will take the parallel video encoder (PVE) component of the DVR case study as an example for illustration.

First, the designer of DVR needs to specify two SysML models for PVE. The state machine diagram and the block definition diagram of PVE (called *PVEEncoding* here) are illustrated in Figs. **5** and **6**, respectively.

As shown in Fig. **5**, the state machine of the *PVEEncoding* class has two states, namely `Idle` and `Encoding`, where `Idle` is the initial state. On receiving the *EncodeOneFrame_SIG* signal, it transits to the `Encoding` state and executes four functions in pipeline, namely preprocessor(), dct(), quan(), and huff(). Preprocessor() gets a raw frame, dct() performs the discrete cosine transform, quan() performs quantization, and huff() performs Huffman encoding. This is the standard image encoding sequence. The It returns to the `Idle` state on receiving the *EncodeOneFrameDone_SIG* signal. Note the `<<pipeline>>` stereotype associated with the state transition from `Idle` to `Encoding`. Associated with this stereotype is a parallel model for pipeline, which needs to be specified by the designer by customizing the design pattern provided by VMC.

As shown in Fig. **6**, the block definition diagram for PVEEncoding includes two parts, namely the private data attributes and the member functions including the constructor and destructor. Note that the designer has to specify all these attributes and functions and also define the functions, that is, write the actual code for the functions.

These two models of PVEEncoding are provided as XML input files to the model parser, which then outputs an XML semantics tree containing all the model related information.

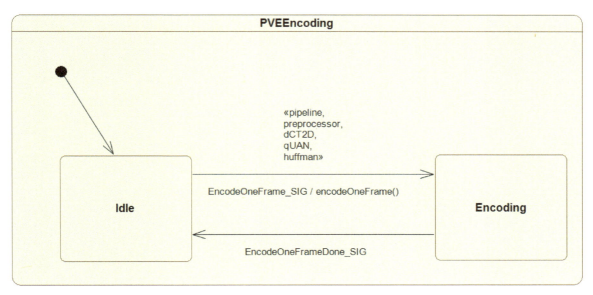

Figure 5: State machine diagram of PVEEncoding.

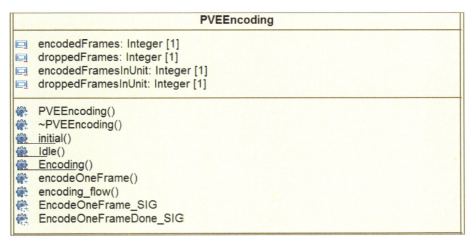

Figure 6: Block definition diagram of PVEEncoding.

Given the semantics tree, the model compiler translates the model artifacts in the user-specified state machine diagrams and block definition diagrams into corresponding pieces of QP code. Each state machine is realized by an *active object* (QActive) in QP, which is similar to the *runnable* class in Java, that is, a class that has a dedicated thread for execution of its behavior. The state machine is declared as a class in C++ and inherits from QActive. VMC provides a QP information file for the detailed mapping from each state and transition in a state machine model into corresponding patterns of QP code. For example, a state corresponds to QState and a transition corresponds to Q_TRAN in QP.

As shown in Fig. **7**, the design flow in the model compiler is accomplished by three parts, namely semantics tree traverser, QP code transformer, and QP code generator. The semantics tree traverser visits all nodes in the semantics tree, the QP code transformer and the QP code generator generate the corresponding QP code.

When the model compiler encounters a node named "*uml:StateMachine,*" it generates the QP initialization code to initialize the active object and signals used in the active object. If the model compiler encounters a node named "*uml:State,*" it generates the corresponding QP code based on the QP information file. When the model compiler encounters a node named "*uml:Transition,*" it generates the corresponding QP code according to the event conditions and actions on the transition.

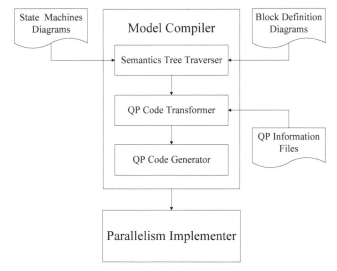

Figure 7: Architecture of Model Compiler.

Finally, each piece of generated QP code is annotated (embedded) in the corresponding node in the semantics tree. The model compiler outputs the QP-annotated tree.

For ease of illustration, we directly show the C++ files generated by the VMC code generator for the QP version of *PVEEncoding*, instead of showing them on the semantics tree. Figs. **8** and **9** illustrate the C++ code generated by the VMC code generator for the PVEEncoding SysML models in Figs. **5** and **6**. Note how the code in PVEEncoding.h conforms to the block definition diagram and the code in PVEEncoding.cpp conforms to the state machine diagram.

Note that during the QP code generation process the <<pipeline>> stereotype was not processed and thus the full pipeline of the four functions is executed solely by the thread of the PVEEncoding active object. Though the functional results are correct, there is no parallelism in the pipeline. Performance is thus limited.

For parallelization of the pipeline, the designer needs to specify a parallel model corresponding to the pipeline stereotype in *PVEEncoding*. Before discussing how the parallel model is to be constructed, we will first describe the architecture of the parallelism implementer in the VMC code generator, which is responsible for parallel code generation. Finally, we will show how the parallelism implementer generates code for data flow parallelism, that is, the parallel pipeline.

```
class PVEEncoding : public QActive
{
public:
    PVEEncoding();
    ~PVEEncoding();
private:
    static QState initial(PVEEncoding* me, QEvent const *e);
    static QState Idle(PVEEncoding* me, QEvent const *e);
    static QState Encoding(PVEEncoding* me, QEvent const *e);
    int encodedFrames;
    int dropedFrames;
    int encodedFramesInUnit;
    int dropedFramesInUnit;
};
```

Figure 8: PVEEncoding.h.

```
static QState PVEEncoding::initial(PVEEncoding* me, QEvent const *e)
{
    me->subscribe(EncodeOneFrame_SIG);
    me->subscribe(EncodeOneFrameDone_SIG);
    return Q_TRAN(&PVEEncoding::Idle);
}


static QState PVEEncoding::Idle(PVEEncoding* me, QEvent const *e)
{
    if( e->sig==EncodeOneFrame_SIG )
    {
        // .....
    }
    return Q_SUPER(&QHsm::top);
}


static QState PVEEncoding::Encoding(PVEEncoding* me, QEvent const *e)
{
    if( e->sig==Q_ENTRY_SIG )
    {
        // .....
    }
    else if( e->sig==EncodeOneFrameDone_SIG )
    {
        // .....
    }
    else if( e->sig==EncodeOneFrame_SIG )
    {
        // .....
    }
    return Q_SUPER(&QHsm::top);
}
```

Figure 9: PVEEncoding.cpp.

As illustrated in Fig. **10**, the parallelism implementer consists of three parts, including QP-annotated tree traverser, parallel model transformer, and TBB code generator. The QP-annotated tree from the model compiler is traversed by the QP-annotated tree traverser such that all nodes tagged with pre-defined stereotypes are identified. The stereotypes are related to parallelization, including task parallelism, data parallelism, and data flow parallelism. The association between each kind of stereotype with a parallel model is found in the TBB information file. For each stereotype found by the traverser, the parallel model transformer identifies the associated user-customized parallel model. Finally, the TBB code generator constructs the pieces of C++ code corresponding to each pair of stereotype and parallel model. These pieces of code contain invocations of the TBB library APIs and are annotated to corresponding nodes in the XML semantics tree. The output of the parallelism implementer is a TBB-annotated tree.

Currently, the VMC code generator uses a SysML profile with stereotypes to support parallel design patterns. Users can apply the following stereotypes: <<*pipeline*>> to a transition of a state machine, <<*serial_filter*>> and <<*parallel_filter*>> to a function invocation on a transition, where a filter is the TBB terminology for a pipeline stage. Using this profile, VMC bridges the gap between model-level and code-level parallelisms.

Recall as shown in Fig. **5,** the stereotype <<*pipeline*>> was applied to the transition between the Idle state and the Encoding state of the PVEEncoding example. Here, <<*pipeline*>> has two serial filters, namely *Preprocessor* that decomposes raw frames for parallel processing by parallel filters and *Huffman* that encodes data blocks and composes encoded frames for transmission to the storage. The other two are parallel filters, namely *DCT2D* and *QUAN*, which are responsible for computing in parallel the discrete cosine transformation and the quantization.

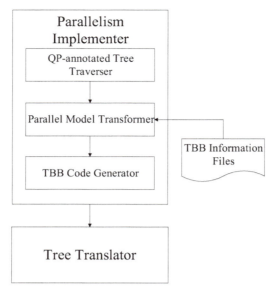

Figure 10: Architecture of parallelism implementer.

The parallel model corresponding to this instance of the <<*pipeline*>> stereotype was specified by the designer as illustrated in Fig. **11**, which includes information for all filters. The sequence of the filters is specified by the sequence of the tagged values appearing in the <<pipeline>> stereotype on the state machine transition, where each tagged value represents the name of a filter in the pipeline.

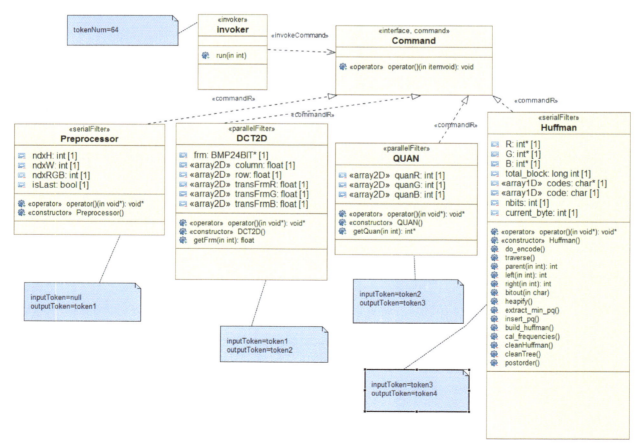

Figure 11: Parallel Model for TBB pipeline.

As an example of the code generation for parallel models, a snippet of code corresponding to the parallel filter, DCT2D, is shown in Fig. **12** and the code for the initialization of the TBB pipeline is shown in Fig. **13**.

As shown in Fig. **12**, the code for the discrete cosine transform is written into the `act_DCT()` function, which is then invoked in the customized `operator()` function. This is a parallel filter, which can be observed from the parameter given to the constructor of DCT2D.

```
class DCT2D : public tbb::filter
{
private:
    UserType parameter;

public:
    DCT2D( UserType param ) : filter(parallel)
    {
        this->parameter = param;
    }

    void* act_DCT( void* item )
    {
        // manually-written code
    }

    void* operator( void* item )
    {
        Token token = <static_cast>(Token*) item;
        return <static_cast>(Token*) act_DCT(token);
    }
};
```

Figure 12: DCT2D.h.

As shown in Fig. **13**, the initialization code needs to instantiate and initialize a TBB task scheduler (`task_scheduler_init`) and a TBB pipeline. The four filters are instantiated and added in sequence to the pipeline. The filter sequence in the pipeline is `Preprocessor`, `DCT2D`, `Quan`, and `Huffman`.

The degree of parallelism in the pipeline can be controlled by changing the total number of tokens (`tokenNum`) used in the pipeline, where a token must be acquired before data can be processed by a filter. A larger number of tokens means increased parallelism, but not necessarily enhanced performance. This is because parallelism is often not without communication overheads, which become performance bottlenecks and thus the overall performance is affected.

Note that each piece of code corresponding to a pair of stereotype and parallel model must be integrated with the transition action code of the corresponding QP active object.

After all pieces of QP active object code and TBB parallel code have been annotated onto the XML semantics tree, the tree translator is used to generate the actual source code files from the TBB-annotated tree. The architecture of the tree translator is depicted in Fig. **14**, which shows that it consists of two parts, namely tree traverser and code generator. The tree traverser visits every node in TBB-annotated tree, and the code generator constructs and writes the source code files into the working directory.

The output files are organized as follows. A `global.h` header file declares all the global variables for the system, including application-specific, QP, and TBB variables. For each system component, a header file defines the SysML block as a QP active object (class) and a program code file defines the state machine, along with all states and transitions. Figs. **8** and **9** illustrate a header file and a program code file for the *PVEEncoding* block. Further, for each parallel pipeline, there is a TBB pipeline initialization source file, as illustrated by Fig. **13**. For each filter in a parallel pipeline, a header file defines the class derived from `tbb::filter`. An example is given in Fig. **12** for the DCT2D filter in the PVE pipeline of DVR.

```
tbb::task_scheduler_init init;
tbb::pipeline ppline;

Preprocessor preprocessor();
DCT2D dct2D();
QUAN quan();
Huffman huffman();

ppline.add_filter(preprocessor();
ppline.add_filter(dct2D);
ppline.add_filter(quan);
ppline.add_filter(huffman);

ppline.run(tokenNum);
ppline.clear();
```

Figure 13: C++ code for TBB pipeline initialization.

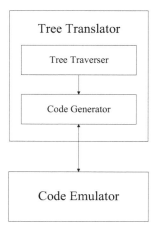

Figure 14: Architecture of Tree Translator.

For ease of compilation, makefiles are automatically generated by VMC for the application. Since platform-related information such as processor type (ARM 11 MPCore), operating system (Linux), state machine library (QP), parallel library (TBB) is specified by the designer at the start of the project, the corresponding makefiles are customized to the platform. Details of this architecture mapping and makefile generation can be found in Chapter 5 of this book.

The code emulator in VMC allows a designer to monitor the status of system execution by automatically instrumenting the application code with additional code for system monitoring. The designer may choose not to include this additional code in the application product after the debugging phase.

As illustrated in Fig. **15**, the code emulator itself is modeled and realized as an additional QP active object called *Monitor* that can monitor all other active objects in the application. The monitor communicates with other active objects periodically, and writes information into the System Information Log file, which can then be used for information display such as using a spreadsheet software tool.

Arbitrary runtime information can be monitored by the code emulator (Monitor), as long as, the monitored component complies with a standard feedback interface provided and supported by VMC called `getInfo()`. Each monitored component QP active object is instrumented with this standard feedback interface so that the code emulator can invoke this interface, whenever required, to retrieve runtime information. The time interval for runtime information retrieval by the code emulator can be set for each component.

For example as shown in Fig. **15**, in the DVR application, the capture rate of all digital cameras (from *PVECapture*), the encoding rate of all video streams (from *PVEEncoding*), the streaming rate of all client connections (from *Encoded Data Buffer Manager*, *i.e.*, EDBM) and the platform-specific CPU core utilizations (via OS system-calls) can be monitored in real-time for each available core in the processor.

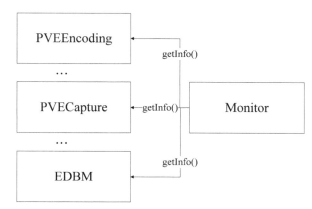

Figure 15: Monitoring in the VMC Code Emulator.

CONCLUSIONS

This chapter reviewed the multi-core software design flow in the code generator of the VERTAF / Multicore (VMC) Framework. A case study on parallel video encoder of a digital video recording system was used to illustrate each step of the code generation process. The flexibility and feasibility of the proposed code generator architecture were demonstrated through the example. Future work will consist of more application development using this VMC code generator and the support for more state machine and parallel libraries such as TPL, OpenMP, etc

REFERENCES

[1]   Cantrill B. and Bonwick J. Real-world concurrency. ACM Queue. 2008; 6(5):16–25.
[2]   Hsiung P.-A., Lin S.-W., Tseng C.-H., *et al.* VERTAF: An Application Framework for the Design and Verification of Embedded Real-Time Software. IEEE Transactions on Software Engineering. 2004; 30: 656-19.
[3]   Hsiung P.-A., Lin S.-W., Chen Y.-R., *et al.* Model-Driven Development of Multi-Core Embedded Software. In: Proceedings of the 2nd International Workshop on Multicore Software Engineering (IWMSE); 2009: Vancouver, Canada: IEEE Computer Society 2009; pp. 9-8.
[4]   Hsiung P.-A., Lin C.-S., Lin S.-W., *et al.* VERTAF/Multi-Core: A SysML-based Application Framework for Multi-Core Embedded Software Development. In: Proceedings of the International Conference on Algorithms and Architectures for Parallel Processing (ICA3PP); 2009: Taipei, Taiwan: LNCS, Springer Verlag 2009; pp. 303-12.
[5]   Lin C.-S., Hsiung P.-A., Lin S.-W., *et al.* VERTAF/Multi-Core: A SysML-based Application Framework for Multi-Core Embedded Software Development. J Chin Instit Engine 2009; 32: 985-7.
[6]   Intel Threading Building Blocks. http://www.threadingbuildingblocks.org/. 2008.
[7]   C.H. Lien, Y. W. Bai, and M.B. Lin. Estimation by software for the power consumption of streaming-media servers. IEEE Transac Instrument Measur 2007; 56(5): 1859-12.
[8]   OpenMP. http://www.openmp.org/. 2008.
[9]   Papyrus UML. http://www.papyrusuml.org/. 2009.
[10]   Reinders J. Intel Threading Building Blocks: Outfitting C++ for Multi-core Processor Parallelism. O'Reilly 2007.
[11]   Samek M. Practical UML StateCharts in C/C++, Second Edition: Event-Driven Programming for Embedded Systems. Newnes, 2008.
[12]   Wang F. and Hsiung P.-A. Efficient and user-friendly verification. IEEE Transac Comput, 51(1):61–83, January 2002.

[13]   System Modeling Language (SysML) 1.1. http://www.omgsysml.org/. 2008.

[14]   Microsoft Task Parallel Library (TPL). http://msdn.microsoft.com/en-us/library/dd460717.aspx. 2007.

[15]   Unified Modeling Language (UML) 2.0. http://www.omg.org/spec/UML/2.0/. 2005.

[16]   Quantum Leaps. http://www.state-machine.com/. 2010.

Index

A

Architecture mapping 63, 68

B

Block definition diagram 65, 66, 68, 69, 78, 80, 82, 84-86

C

CACP See Conflict-Aware Assignment with Conflict Priority
CAWP See Conflict-Aware Assignment with Workload Priority
Chip Multiprocessor 33
Class diagram 62, 78
Conflict-Aware Assignment with Conflict Priority
Conflict-Aware Assignment with Workload Priority 42
CMP See Chip Multiprocessor
Code generator 78-80, 82-89, 91
Code generation 62-64, 68, 76, 78-80, 82, 86, 89, 91, 63, 68
Code optimization 63, 69
Code testing 63, 69
Core Degree 48

D

D-Cache 33
D-Page See Data-Page
Data Page 38
Design modeling 63, 66
Digital Video Recording 61, 73, 76, 78-80, 91
Dynamic Voltage Scaling 35
DVS See Dynamic Voltage Scaling
DVR See Digital Video Recording

E

Embedded software 61-64, 68, 69, 76, 78, 80, 81, 91
Embedded system 3, 21, 25, 31, 59, 61, 62, 68, 69, 73, 76, 78, 80, 81, 92

G

GoF style 66
GPGPU 33

I

I-TLB See Instruction-TLB
I-Cache 33
I-Page See Instruction-Page
ILP See Instruction-Level Parallelism
Instruction-Level Parallelism 39
Instruction-Page 37
Instruction-TLB 36

M

Many-core processors 3, 4, 6, 14-16
MDA See model-driven architecture
Miss table 22, 23, 26, 29
Model-driven architecture 61
Model repository 63, 72
Multi-core processor 33, 34, 36, 38-41, 43, 44, 47-51, 58, 61, 62, 69, 76, 78, 81, 92

O

OpenMP 61, 62, 69

P

PAE See Physical Address Extension
Parallel code 78, 80-82, 84, 86, 89
Performance 3-7, 9, 13, 16, 19-22, 24-26, 29, 33, 34, 36, 39, 46-51, 53, 55-58, 61, 62, 69, 70, 73, 74, 76, 81, 83, 86, 89
Physical Address Extension 35
Physical Page Number 36
Physically-Indexed Physically-Tagged 36
PIPT See Physically-Indexed Physically-Tagged
Power 3-6, 9, 14, 16, 19-22, 24-29, 33-35, 61, 73, 75, 76, 81
PPN See Physical Page Number

Q

QP See Quantum Platform
Quantum Platform 61, 62, 68, 69, 73-77, 80-82, 84-91

R

Random Assignment with No Priority 42
RANP See Random Assignment with No Priority
Requirements modeling 63, 64

S

SCTR See Single-Core Tag Reduction
SGM See State Graph Manipulators
Shared Memory Multiprocessor 39
Single-Core Tag Reduction 44
SMP See Shared Memory Multiprocessor
State Graph Manipulators 62, 68, 76
State machine diagram 78, 82, 84-86
SysML See System Modeling Language
System Modeling Language (SysML) 61-65, 68, 69, 73, 76-80, 82, 84, 86, 87, 89, 91, 92

T

Tag Reduction 33
Tag Reduction on Chip Multiprocessor 33
TBB See Threading Building Blocks